To: Ralph

Merry Christmas, 1993

Love,
Johnny & Wanda

Kentucky's
Road to Statehood

Ordered that the constitution with the amendments thereto
be fairly transcribed and entered at large on the journals &
read again Tomorrow which is in the following words
Viz:

We the Representatives of the people of
the State of Kentucky in Convention assembled
do ordain and establish this Constitution for its Government.

Article I.

The powers of Government shall be divided into
three distinct departments, each of them to be confided
to a Separate body of magistracy, to wit, those which are
legislative to one, those which are executive to another,
and those which are judiciary to another.

No person or collection of persons being of one of these
departments shall exercise any power properly belonging
to either of the others, except in the instances hereinafter
expressly permitted.

The legislative power of this commonwealth
shall be vested in a general Assembly which shall
consist of a Senate and house of representatives.

The representatives shall be chosen annually
by the qualified electors of each County respectively,
on the first tuesday in may; but the severall elections
may be continued for three days, if, in the opinion of
the presiding officer, or officers, it shall be necessary,
and no longer.

Kentucky's Road to Statehood

Lowell H. Harrison

THE UNIVERSITY PRESS OF KENTUCKY

Frontispiece: Draft of the first page of the Kentucky
Constitution of 1792, from the journal of the Tenth
Convention. Courtesy of the Kentucky Historical Society.

Copyright © 1992 by The University Press of Kentucky

Scholarly publisher for the Commonwealth,
serving Bellarmine College, Berea College, Centre
College of Kentucky, Eastern Kentucky University,
The Filson Club, Georgetown College, Kentucky
Historical Society, Kentucky State University,
Morehead State University, Murray State University,
Northern Kentucky University, Transylvania University,
University of Kentucky, University of Louisville,
and Western Kentucky University.

Editorial and Sales Offices: Lexington, Kentucky 40508-4008

Library of Congress Cataloging-in-Publication Data
Harrison, Lowell Hayes, 1922-
    Kentucky's road to statehood / Lowell H. Harrison.
        p.   cm.
    Includes bibliographical references and index.
    ISBN 0-8131-1782-8
    1. Kentucky—Politics and government—To 1792. 2. Kentucky—
Constitutional history.   3. Statehood (American politics)—
History—18th Century.   I. Title.
F455.H37   1992
976.9'02—dc20   91-34642

This book is printed on recycled acid-free paper meeting
the requirements of the American National Standard
for Permanence of Paper for Printed Library Materials.
                            ∞

Contents

List of Illustrations   vii

Preface   ix

1. Stirrings of Discontent   1

2. The Early Conventions   19

3. A Spanish Conspiracy?   48

4. The Later Conventions   73

5. Writing the Constitution   93

6. The Constitution Achieved   115

7. Implementing the Constitution   131

Appendix A. The Formation of Counties, 1780-1792   149

Appendix B. Chronology: Major Events on the
Road to Statehood   150

Appendix C. The Kentucky Constitution of 1792   152

Notes   169

Bibliographical Note   185

Index   194

Illustrations

James Wilkinson   33
Humphrey Marshall   37
Mercer County Courthouse   39
Grayson's Tavern   40
Harry Innes   52
George Nicholas   76
Isaac Shelby   135

Preface

While a great deal has been written about Kentucky during the pioneer and formative eras, surprisingly little has been done in recent years on the separation from Virginia and the creation of the Commonwealth of Kentucky. Historians have tended to move quickly from Daniel Boone to Henry Clay, from the Indian attacks on the isolated stations to the War of 1812. Little attention has been paid to some critical developments in the intervening years. With the bicentennial of statehood rapidly approaching, this is an appropriate time to take another look at the long and sometimes rocky road to statehood. It is well to recall those years, for many of the roots of our present society rest in that early soil.

This is not a general history of Kentucky during the 1784-1792 period. While I have attempted, within the confines of length, to discuss events in the context of their time, many important developments during those years that do not relate directly to the movement for statehood are merely alluded to or ignored. This investigation attempts to answer four major questions about the statehood movement. Why did Kentuckians seek separation from Virginia? Why did the interminable process take ten conventions and nearly as many years? What were the roles of James Wilkinson and the Spanish Conspiracy? When statehood was at last achieved, what type of government did Kentucky establish? This study begins with the separation sentiment before the first convention in 1784; it concludes with the selection of Frankfort as the state capital following the first session of the General Assembly in 1792.

Many persons have helped with the work on this project. Nancy Baird, Constance Mills, and other staff members of the Kentucky Library at Western Kentucky University, where much of the research was done, went beyond duty to find elusive materials and to create a pleasant working environment. Mary Margaret Bell, Kentucky Historical Society, and James J. Holmberg, The Filson Club, were generous in sharing their knowledge of their respective manuscript collections. Also very helpful were the staffs at Special Collections at the University of Kentucky, Special Collections at the University of Chicago, and the Manuscript Division of the Library of Congress. Mary Jane Kinsman of The Filson Club, Lisa M. Parrott of the J.B. Speed Art Museum, Louisville, and Jean E. Unglaub of the Kentucky Department of Parks were generous in their efforts to find possible illustrations. Susan Gore, Interlibrary Loans, Western Kentucky University Libraries, was always diligent in obtaining needed materials. The Western Kentucky University Faculty Research Fund provided welcome assistance for travel and the duplication of materials. I am grateful for the support the Department of History has given a retired member, and I have special thanks for Elizabeth Jensen, the departmental secretary, who always knew the right key to strike.

Particular thanks go to my wife, Penny Harrison, who has supported my research and writing in so many ways.

ONE

Stirrings of Discontent

George Rogers Clark may have been the first Kentuckian to warn Virginia that its western inhabitants might separate from the Old Dominion. With the American Revolution in progress in 1776, Kentucky's status was uncertain, and Clark decided to take advantage of that situation. "I immediately fixed on my plans," he wrote in his memoirs, "that of assembling the people, get them to elect deputies and send them to the Assembly of Virginia and treat with them respecting the Country. If valuable conditions were procured, to declare ourselves citizens of the state, otherways, establish an independent government, and, by giving away great part of the lands and disposing of the remainder otherways, we could not only gain great numbers of inhabitants, but in good measure protect them." [1]

Instead of following Clark's plan, those attending a meeting at Harrodsburg in June 1776 elected the absent Clark and John Gabriel Jones as delegates to ask the state government to name Kentucky a county. While they waited for the General Assembly to convene, Clark presented Kentucky's desperate need for gunpowder to Governor Patrick Henry. The governor referred him to the Executive Council, which expressed sympathy for their "Friends in Distress" but said they could not give the powder to "a detached people . . . not yet united to the state of Virginia." Clark replied that he could not accept the powder as a loan, that he was "sorry to find that we should have to seek protection else whare, which I did not doubt of getting; that if a Cuntrey was not worth protecting, it was not worth claiming."[2] Faced with that threat, the Council reconsidered, and on August 23, 1776, it gave de facto recognition to Kentucky by ordering 500 pounds of gunpowder delivered to Clark for the defense of the western settlers.[3]

Clark had already helped block the attempt by Judge Richard Henderson and his Transylvania Company associates to establish a colony that would take from Virginia much of the area that eventually became the state of Kentucky. Lacking a royal charter, the company negotiated the Treaty of Sycamore Shoals with the Cherokees in the spring of 1775. In return for some £10,000 in trade goods and sterling, the company received title to the lands lying inside a rough triangle formed by the Ohio, Cumberland, and Kentucky rivers. Before the treaty was actually signed, Daniel Boone led a band of axemen to open the Wilderness Trace into the heart of Kentucky. Henderson followed to establish a settlement and to start disposing of the millions of acres the company claimed. He hoped and expected that the British government would accept the company's ownership. The American Revolution negated that expectation, and the new states of Virginia and North Carolina rejected Henderson's claims to their lands.

Henderson did have some success with early land sales, although there were complaints that his prices were exorbitant, and several stations besides Boonesborough were established in the area the company claimed. A government would strengthen the company's claim and add stability to the region, so on May 23 delegates from several small stations assembled under a giant elm at Boonesborough. There they adopted nine measures that established courts, provided for the punishment of crimes, set fees for sheriffs and clerks, and attempted to preserve the range and wild game and to improve the breeds of horses. The next day Henderson and the delegates signed a covenant that provided for a government with powers shared between the company and the settlers. Scheduled to meet again on the first Thursday in September, this embryonic legislature never reassembled.

Critics of the Transylvania Company charged that its scheme violated the charter rights of Virginia, a Virginia act of 1705 that forbade a private citizen to purchase land from Indians, the Proclamation of 1763 that prohibited settlement beyond the crest of the mountains, and the Treaty of Fort Stanwix (1768), in which the Iroquois Confederation ceded its claims to the Kentucky area to the British crown. Some of the early settlers were unhappy with both the high prices the company charged and their uncertain titles; they believed that cheaper and more secure lands could be obtained if Virginia was the owner. Benjamin Logan was only one of the leaders of the early settlers who soon quarreled with Henderson, and Clark worked actively to kill Henderson's scheme. Final rejection came in December 1776, when Virginia's General Assembly created Kentucky County. Virginia later gave Henderson a grant of 200,000 acres near the mouth of the Green River in recognition of his services in promoting early settlement.[4] It was a far cry from the empire of which he had dreamed.

As the Council indicated to Clark, there had been uncertainty about Kentucky's status. The 1609 charter had given the London Company all lands within the bounds of two hundred miles north and two hundred miles south of Old Point Comfort, "from sea to sea, west and northwest." Those boundaries could be interpreted in several ways, but the way generally accepted in Virginia gave the colony claim to nearly half the North American continent. The Proclamation of 1763, however, suggested that the crown might rescind the sea-to-sea provision and set the western boundary at the crest of the mountains. The expulsion of the French from North America at the end of the French and Indian War in 1763 made western settlement more feasible than it had been. Various land companies and ambitious individuals attempted to secure charters that would have violated Virginia's claims to ownership of the lands on the western waters.

After the outbreak of the Revolution, the Second Continental Congress became the national government until 1781, when the Articles of Confederation replaced it. Neither government had the power to tax, and the creation of a public domain

in the largely unoccupied West offered a way of securing des-
perately needed revenue. Ratification of the Articles was blocked until the states with western claims agreed to relinquish at
least part of their claims to the central government. Meanwhile, Virginia had created Kentucky County, and when Virginia gave up its claims it abandoned only the land north of the
Ohio River. Even there the state reserved enough acres to pay
George Rogers Clark and his men for their military service.
The peace treaty of 1783 established the Mississippi River as
the western boundary of the new republic.

Most Virginians, including those already living in Kentucky, believed that the transmontane would inevitably break
away from the parent state. The Virginia constitution of 1776
provided for separation, and Kentucky was so isolated in distance and time that the eastern and western parts of the state
saw problems and issues from quite different perspectives.
While the Kentucky population was small, matters could go
unattended without creating too much disturbance, but immigration into Kentucky increased sharply even before the end of
the war, and it grew even more rapidly after the British sur-
render at Yorktown.

As Kentuckians began to ponder their political future they
saw four major options. They could remain a part of Virginia
and hope that as they grew the state government would pay
more attention to their needs. Their representation in the General Assembly would increase as new counties were created,
and so would their political clout. Some Kentuckians with
strong ties to the Old Dominion, even if only sentimental ones,
hesitated to break away. They were familiar with the existing
relationship; was improvement sure if they changed government?

A second faction favored separation if it could be achieved
with Virginia's consent and on mutually agreed terms. This
procedure had been outlined in the 1776 constitution, and they
assumed that separation would be followed by admission to
the Union. Kentucky landowners with Virginia titles tended to
favor this approach, for the required agreement would protect
their holdings.

A third group, more impatient than the second, saw no

need to seek Virginia's approval and to work out terms of separation. They favored calling a convention in Kentucky that would unilaterally declare independence. The new state would then be free to adopt the land and other policies that would be most favorable to its people. At least some of the large Virginia land grants might be canceled. Ultimately, Kentucky would seek admission to the Union.

The fourth and most radical group favored the course that Clark had suggested. Kentucky should declare independence, then negotiate an association with some foreign power. It might be the United States, but it might be a European power. For years after the peace treaty was signed, Great Britain retained posts on American soil north of the Ohio River and indicated interest in retarding the western movement in the United States. Support of the British navy would help insure the free use of the Mississippi River and the port of New Orleans. But, since Spain controlled the mouth of the Mississippi, a Spanish association would have distinct advantages. Yet many Kentuckians were adamantly opposed to any foreign relationship.

Immigration was an important aspect of the separation movement, for a sizable population was needed to command serious attention from Virginia and the United States. Reliable statistics are not available before the 1790 census, but in the spring of 1775, as the first permanent settlements were being started, the total was probably about 150, all of them men. Most of them came to Kentucky in search of good land, although some were attracted by the lure of adventure. Even before the first settlements were founded, Kentucky was known on the Atlantic seaboard and in Europe as a veritable Garden of Eden, a lovely enchanted land that "connoted abundance in all desirable things and boundless liberty for all." The shining aspirations and expectations that had faded before the realities of earlier frontiers were renewed in Kentucky, and a myth developed that continued to symbolize the American frontier long after it had vanished.[5] Lewis Craig spoke for many Kentuckians when he asserted that "Heaven is a mere Kentucky of a place."[6]

Many of the early settlers were Scotch-Irish from Virginia,

Pennsylvania, and North Carolina. Daniel Boone, James Harrod, and Benjamin Logan were among the pioneer leaders who came early and held the land against all odds. George Rogers Clark, unmarried and primarily a soldier, did not fit into their pattern. The Indian danger forced the early settlers to spend more time in the small stations or forts than they wished. They wanted and needed to live and work on the acres they had claimed. Instead, half of them might work in fields adjacent to the fort while the other half stood guard with their Kentucky rifles. Precious livestock shared space in the cramped stations, for Indians, if given an opportunity, would kill the cattle and take the horses. Especially during the cooped-up winter months, overcrowded, unsanitary conditions led to disease, discontent, and quarrels. When William Fleming reached Boonesborough in December 1779, he commented in his diary: "The Fort is a dirty place in winter like every other Station."[7] These pioneers were almost uniformly convinced that Virginia neglected their needs, especially in regard to Indian defense.

Clark's limited success in the Illinois region in 1778-1779 reduced the Indian danger and encouraged immigration into Kentucky. By then most of the fighting along the eastern seaboard had shifted to the southern states, and many of the newcomers were refugees from a bitter civil war. Most of them were patriots or at least neutrals, but an appreciable number were Tories who could expect persecution from their neighbors if no British troops were in the vicinity to provide protection. William Clinkenbeard exaggerated when he recalled highlights of his trip through the Wilderness in the winter of 1778-1779: "Everybody coming to Kentucky. Could hardly get along the road for them; and all grand Tories, pretty nigh. All from Carolina [were] Tories. Had been treated so bad there, they had to run off or do worse." He added that later he was sent to Boonesborough to help guard the Tories there.[8] Suspicions were so great that even Daniel Boone was tried (but acquitted) for alleged Tory activities. Indians seldom checked political affiliations before attacking, and, faced with that common danger, most Tories soon merged into the general population, to which they added a somewhat conservative outlook.

Immigration increased so sharply in 1778-1779 that General Lachan McIntosh at Pittsburgh wrote General George Washington that "the immigration down the Ohio from this quarter I fear will depopulate it altogether." John Floyd at the Falls of the Ohio reported in the spring of 1780 that "near 300 large boats have arrived this spring at the Falls with families. . . . We have six stations on Beargrass with not less than 600 men." Most surprising were the ten to fifteen wagons that could be seen daily on the dirt roads near the Falls. Among the unusual overland parties in 1781 was a Baptist congregation called the "Travelling Church." Led by the Reverend Lewis Craig, they moved as a group from Spotsylvania County, Virginia.[9]

Some observers believed that they detected a change in the character and caliber of the newcomers. The lure of adventure was obviously less important than it had been in the early days of settlement. Many, perhaps most, of the new immigrants were poor people who hoped to find good, cheap land or were fleeing from taxation or military service. A more diverse group than their predecessors had been, they represented every state and a number of foreign countries. A careful study of the 1790 tax rolls concluded that 51.6 percent of Kentuckians were of English descent, a figure below the national average of 57.1 percent. Scots and Scotch-Irish were 24.8 percent, the Irish were 9 percent, the Welsh were 6.7 percent, and the Germans were 4.9 percent. Caleb Wallace assured James Madison in 1785 that Kentucky was "a good poor man's country," but many of Wallace's fellow Kentuckians would have disagreed with him.[10] When they discovered that land was no longer free and that most good land had been taken, many of the newcomers joined the ranks of the discontented. As they blamed the Richmond government for their plight, they wondered if they might not have better prospects under another government. They could hardly be worse off.

Immigration declined after the 1779-1780 surge, then increased again in 1784. The long war had ended at last, and Virginia was discharging its debts to its soldiers with land warrants based upon military service, including the rank held. The military warrants had to be located in the West, and so many people moved to Kentucky in 1784 that the population may have nearly doubled that year. A report to the British government estimated the 1788 Kentucky population at 62,000, and the 1790 census reported 73,677 persons.

Until near the turn of the century more immigrants entered Kentucky through the Cumberland Gap than came down the Ohio River. No wheeled vehicle is known to have gone over the Wilderness Trace until well after statehood. Heavily laden packhorses carried goods along the tortuous trail; many of the prospective settlers walked. The Ohio River route also had Indian dangers in addition to its navigational hazards, but a major drawback was the distance that often had to be covered before the traveler reached the Ohio or one of its tributaries. Flatboats were expensive to buy and hard to build when one was impatient to move on, but they could carry a large cargo of household goods as well as people and animals.

Pioneer Kentucky changed rapidly under the human onslaught. John A. McClung, an early Kentucky historian who was familiar with the post-Revolutionary scene, wrote that "The hunters of the elk and buffalo were now succeeded by the more ravenous hunters of land; in the pursuit, they fearlessly braved the hatchet of the Indian and the privations of the forest." [11] Within a few years the Indian threat diminished in Kentucky and much of the great forest gave way to cultivated fields.

Another change was noted in the composition of the immigrants in the mid-1780s. Historian Temple Bodley was convinced that those who were starting to come in 1784 were far superior to those who had come in 1780. While a broad spectrum of social and economic classes was represented, Bodley said that in 1784 there were "many families of high social position in the east, and many men of eminent ability and reputation." Many in this group were from the Valley of Virginia, and a number of them had held civil or military offices. [12] Their arrival contributed to a sharp change of leadership in Kentucky. From the first convention in 1784 to statehood in 1792, the leaders of the separation movement were almost totally different from the leaders of the pioneer years. The Clarks, Boones, Harrods, and Kentons had little impact on the decisions made at the ten conventions. Benjamin Logan was the main exception, for he did have a substantial role in both the conventions and the new state government of the 1790s. Isaac Shelby also spanned both periods, but he did not make Kentucky his home until near the end of 1782.

The rapid growth of population ended the frontier stage very quickly in much of Kentucky, and the buckskin-clad pioneers disappeared with it. As a future president of the United States once wrote, "The frontiersman destroys the wilderness, and yet its destruction means his own."[13] By 1784, with the Indian danger abated if not ended, farmers produced their first substantial market crops. The towns were growing rapidly, and the appearance of such amenities as stores, schools, horse races, and distilleries proved the arrival of civilization. Ann Wilkinson wrote her father from Lexington on September 25, 1789: "It is astonishing how fast this Town improves. It is by far the largest in the District & it is expected the Emigration this fall will be greater than ever. Report says there are Seventy familys in the Wilderness now on there [*sic*] way to Kentucky."[14] The 1790 census credited Lexington with 834 inhabitants.

Kentucky's increase in population caused the Virginia government to make several political changes. For many years, first as a colony and then as a state, Virginia had included its frontier holdings in an enormous country; adjustments were made as the frontier settlements moved westward. In 1772 the area that became Kentucky was a part of Fincastle County. Four years later Montgomery, Washington, and Kentucky counties were formed. By 1780 Kentucky's growth justified its division into Lincoln, Jefferson, and Fayette counties, and a start had been made toward the ultimate appalling total of 120 county units. The region then became known as the District of Kentucky. Before statehood was achieved, Nelson (1784), Bourbon, Madison, and Mercer (1785), and Woodford and Mason (1788) counties had also been added. Each county sent two representatives to the lower house of the legislature, but Richmond was so distant that men often shunned election. Even with the increased representation, Kentuckians were in such a minority that they often complained they could not secure redress for western grievances.

The creation of a county meant the appointment of justices of the peace and the opening of county and quarter session courts. In 1782 the General Assembly, recognizing that "the mode of administrating justice has become exceedingly inconvenient and burthensome to suitors being westwardly of the Allegheny mountains," created a supreme court for the Kentucky District. The first federal court in Kentucky was formed by the Judiciary Act of 1789, one of the major acts passed by the First Congress under the new constitution. It provided a federal district court for each of the eleven states that had ratified the constitution and for the districts of Maine and Kentucky. Harry Innes left his state position to accept the federal post he was to hold for twenty-seven years. His duties were not arduous during the court's early years. Not until 1799 did its docket list as many as twenty cases, and Innes continued his private legal practice.[15]

The establishment of the courts with their judges, clerks, and district attorneys made an important contribution to Kentucky's development. The courts reflected both the population growth of the region and the litigious nature of its society. They brought to Kentucky a small but influential group of men who provided much of the leadership so urgently needed. Relatively well educated, usually young and ambitious, they formed the nucleus of the political faction that became known as the court party.

Most of the court cases involved the incredibly complex land claims. The systematic survey that was done in the Northwest Territory was not applied to Kentucky, and the haphazard location of tracts resulted in many shingled claims that complicated titles for future generations. Some limited surveying was done before Lord Dunmore's War (1774) to provide payment to Virginians who had fought in the French and Indian War. The Transylvania Company failed to get most of Kentucky, but Virginia accepted the validity of several hundred claims on land purchased from the company. By 1776 three types of land claims existed in Kentucky: military service claims, Transylvania Company claims, and squatters' claims that had no legal basis. On June 24, 1776, the Virginia Convention that was directing the transition from colony to statehood decided to give preference to the men who had actually settled in Kentucky. An implementing act passed in October granted 400 acres to anyone who had settled in the area before the June 24 decision provided he had been there for a year or had raised a corn crop. The famous land act of 1779 gave 400 acres and a 1,000-acre preemption to each settler who had been in the district for a year prior to January 1778 or who had raised a corn crop. A cabin or hut had to be built before the preemption could be claimed. Lands claimed after January 1778 were to be judged by a special Court of Land Commissioners created that year.

Future titles to land were to be obtained by either military or treasury warrants, with the land south of the Green River reserved for grants to Revolutionary War soldiers. Treasury warrants were purchased at £40 per 100 acres in the inflated currency of the day. A buyer would deposit his money at Richmond and receive a warrant that specified the number of acres and authorized the county surveyor to make the required survey where the purchaser indicated. The resultant plat and survey certificate had to be deposited in Richmond within a year; in due time a deed would be issued. Once payments were required, the average size of Kentucky holdings began to decrease. An act of May 1781, limited to two years but later extended by six months, authorized county courts to order surveys made for settlers too poor to pay for them. A family could get 400 acres at a price of only 20 shillings per 100 acres; this price was reduced to 13 shillings when the extension was granted.[16]

The basic 1779 land act appeared comprehensive and rational, but Mann Butler, one of Kentucky's early historians, declared that "never was a measure of legislation so fruitful of curses and calamities to any community of people as the land law of Kentucky. It has proved a perfect Pandora's box to Kentucky, constantly tricking her industrious and enterprising citizens out of the fruits of their brave and hardy exertions;

distracting our courts and legislatures with its endless per-
plexities and refinements." A major problem was that most of
the good lands were claimed early, often in huge tracts, so that
settlers who came later found it difficult to obtain the land that
had lured them westward. Statistics on landownership are
incomplete, but by the early 1790s a majority of Kentucky
males probably did not own land.[17] One solution was to break
up the large holdings, only a fraction of which were under
cultivation.

Dissatisfaction with the land situation was only one of the
grievances that irked Kentucky's settlers. They were not satisfied by the creation of counties and the establishment of local
courts; the seat of state government was still so remote as to
deny them the benefits of government. The easterners appeared insensitive to western problems, and by the close of the
1770s some of the discontented advocated the separation that
George Rogers Clark had threatened a few years earlier. Petitions were an obvious way to express dissatisfaction and demand redress. One of the most impressive petitions of the early
stage of the separation movement was signed by over 600
inhabitants of Kentucky and the Illinois County that had been
created in 1778. In May 1780 the memorialists asked Congress
to "take Proper Methods to form us into a Separate State," one
that presumably would occupy both banks of the Ohio River.[18]
Congress, beset by innumerable wartime problems and crit-
ically hampered by a dearth of power, ignored this and similar
requests. Since the political future of the nation and states was
still in doubt, that was the only practical response at the time.
It did not satisfy a growing number of Kentuckians.

This early separation movement would have had a better
chance of success had George Rogers Clark agreed to lead it.
Still the most popular figure in the West, he wrote his father on
April 23, 1780, that "The partisans in these counties are again
soliciting me to lead them as their Governor-General, as all
from foreign states are for a new government; but my duty
obliging me to suppress all such proceedings I shall conse-
quently lose the interest of that party." The partisans to whom
he referred were called "designing and perverse members of

Society" who wanted land titles made under Virginia's jurisdiction declared void.[19] "They were a discontent few, most of
whom had no lands," a Kentuckian later recalled, "and assembled for the *purpose of petitioning Congress* to take from
Commonwealth of Virginia *Kentucky* lands and distribute
them on a manner to them (these malcontents) more agreeable."[20]

The partisans' cause was aided in 1780 by the appearance
of *The Public Good*, a pamphlet from Thomas Paine's facile
pen. Author of the famous *Common Sense* pamphlet that had
helped lead the colonists to their Declaration of Independence,
Paine now argued that Virginia did not have a valid claim to its
western lands. He insisted that when the Proclamation of 1763
placed the colony's western boundary at the crest of the mountains, the area west of the line had reverted to the crown. Even
if Virginia did own the transmontane region, Paine asserted,
the state's best policy would be to form a new state from it.
"The present settlers being beyond her reach, and her supposed authority remaining in herself, they will appear to her as
revolters, and she to them as oppressors; and they will produce
such a spirit of mutual dislike, that in a little time a total
disagreement will take place, to the disadvantage of both."
Two years later a petition from a relatively satisfied Kentucky
group charged that Paine's "Inflammentary Pamphlet" was
exciting the people, but a petition of August 27, 1782, followed
Paine's argument. The petitioners insisted that when the 1609
charter was dissolved the western lands had reverted to the
crown; then the Revolution had given those lands to the national government. They respectfully requested that Congress
grant Kentucky statehood. Two years earlier such agitation
had alarmed Governor Thomas Jefferson, who feared that a
successful separation movement in Kentucky might cause the
nation to lose all of its western lands.[21]

In 1784 two Pennsylvania agitators, Joseph Galloway and
George Pomeroy, came to Kentucky. As a future Federalist saw
their activities, they tried "to propagate their seditious doc-
trines, and to overturn the Virginia titles to the land." Inspired
by their rhetoric, some of the landless men in the Lexington

area were reported to have moved onto unoccupied acres. Alarmed conservatives had Galloway tried under an old colonial law for "propagators of false views, to the disturbance of the good people of the colony." Found guilty and fined 1,000 pounds of tobacco, which he could not pay, Galloway was freed on his promise to leave Kentucky at once. Pomeroy, also found guilty, faced a considerably larger fine; he too agreed to leave the region.[22]

The hasty departures of Galloway and Pomeroy did not end the agitation for statehood. Landowners were perhaps most concerned about the validity of their titles, but few could deny that there were other serious problems in the relationship between the Virginia government and the settlers in the West. Most of them were based upon Kentucky's isolation in terms of both miles and time from the seat of Virginia's government, which after April 1780 was Richmond. The grievances were very similar to those of the American colonists prior to the outbreak of the Revolution, although no governor occupied the unenviable status of George III. "We conceive the People of this District do not at present enjoy a greater portion of Liberty than an American Colony might have done a few years ago had she been allowed a Representation in the British Parliament," Caleb Wallace told his friend James Madison.[23] Several hundred miles separated Richmond from Danville, the village that for a decade was the political center of Kentucky. Not only were the miles numerous; many of them were difficult and often dangerous. Not until the mid-1790s did the Kentucky legislature authorize the making of a wagon road through Cumberland Gap. "Over that trail Kentucky traveled to statehood," historian John Caruso has written,[24] but many who started on the Wilderness trek never completed the journey. Few travelers dared risk the Indian danger alone, but even sizable parties (usually numbered in terms of available guns) were at considerable risk. In October 1786 a party of thirty was attacked; twenty-one were killed and five women were captured. Confronted by the dangers and difficulties of the Wilderness, some would-be settlers turned back, but most of them pushed on. A man who made the trip in the mid-1780s wrote that the people he encountered on the trail "seemed absolutely infatuated by something like the old crusading spirit to the holy land."[25] Paradise lay somewhere beyond Cumberland Gap.

Indian policy was one of the most important areas of disagreement between eastern and western Virginia. Kentuckians who lived under constant danger from the Indians were convinced that their best protection lay in preemptive raids against the hostile tribes in their homelands. But offensive action outside the state's boundaries could not be conducted without prior permission from state authorities. Because of the slow communications, permission could not be obtained in time to be effective, yet the Virginia government never provided enough men and resources to protect the Kentucky settlers. After he returned to Kentucky from his Illinois campaign, Clark was bitterly criticized because he could not prevent Indian raiding parties from crossing the Ohio River. To many Kentuckians, the Indian problem was literally a matter of life or death; they were convinced that their state government did not view the problem that seriously.

The distance from Richmond also effectively prevented Kentuckians from appealing decisions rendered in their local courts. A litigant who wanted to appeal had to make the long and dangerous trip back east, then be prepared to wait until the appeal was finally heard. Few Kentuckians could afford to make that kind of investment, and they complained of being denied the justice that was available to the Virginians who lived east of the mountains.

Virginia was also accused of neglecting administration in the West. No provision had been made to extend postal services to Kentucky, and the westerners were often unaware of new laws until months after they had gone into effect. In 1785 William Breckinridge asked his brother, who was expected to come to Kentucky in the near future, to bring copies of the acts of the last General Assembly, "for we are amazedly at a loss for them in this Country for I have scarcely seen one Act of Assembly in this Country. . . . our Country is in a manner left without laws."[26] Several months were required to get an answer from the governor or other state officials. Although the westerners often benefitted from the system of benign neglect, they complained quickly when they wanted something from their government and did not get it.

Since most Kentuckians had been lured westward by a hunger for good land, they were especially sensitive to the state's land laws. Many of the landless settlers were convinced that they were entitled to grants because of their contributions to the defense of the region and their labors in preparing the land for cultivation. Even if it was often evaded, large landholders were enraged by the act of 1782 that imposed a tax of five shillings per 100 acres on patents for treasury warrants on tracts of over 1,400 acres. Christopher Greenup wrote Charles Simms on July 19, 1785, that "the people here are a good deal enraged at the Government of Virginia which I expect will force us to a Separation sooner than we are prepared for it."[27] Because Virginia had not provided for a systematic survey prior to settlement, land titles in Kentucky were in a chaotic condition that supported lawyers for generations to come. An anonymous letter writer commented accurately on the Kentucky land situation in a letter published in the *Maryland Journal* of April 4, 1786: "Whoever purchases there, is sure to purchase a lawsuit."[28] Victims of land disputes often blamed the state government for their plight. A special Land Court held eight terms in various Kentucky towns in 1779-1780 and rendered decisions in over 1,400 cases, but these were only some of the disputed titles, and the court's decisions left many unhappy claimants.[29] Many Kentuckians became convinced that their interests would be served best by a new state government that was located in Kentucky.

As problems continued unsolved, even some loyal Virginians began to ask if changes were not needed. John Marshall, the future Chief Justice of the United States, remained in the East, but his parents and numerous friends moved to Kentucky, and he had a keen interest in its welfare. "I begin to think that the time for a separation is fast approaching," he wrote his friend George Muter on January 7, 1785, "and has perhaps actually arrived." He hoped that it could be achieved "with wisdom and temperance."[30] Others were not so sanguine of what the future might bring. James Speed feared that seditious ideas had spread until "ere long we shall revolt from Government in order to try if we can govern ourselves, which in my opinion, will be jumping out of the frying Pan into the Fire."[31]

A petition of June 1, 1782, one of many addressed to the state and Congress during these years, praised the state government and expressed confidence in its good will. "We know by experience that Kentucky has friends in your house," the petitioners asserted. They asked for better land laws and the establishment of a superior court in the district, but they looked beyond near goals to a harmonious severance of their relationship. "These regulations we have, will carry us toward that stage of maturity when with the tenderness of a kind parent to a departing child, you will direct us to form a constitution and act for ourselves."[32] A growing number of Kentuckians who were not partisans were becoming convinced that the time for separation had arrived. Most of them wanted it to occur with the consent and good will of Virginia and with mutual agreement on terms that would protect their Virginia land titles. Most eastern Virginians agreed with that position. If the state's rights were protected, opposition to Kentucky's detachment would be minor. Indeed, it might be a relief to get rid of the flow of complaints from beyond the mountains.

While Kentuckians disagreed on the best solutions to their problems, the one issue on which practically all of them could unite was the use of the Mississippi River. Under existing conditions, that great river and its tributaries provided the only practical outlet for any commercial surpluses that the westerners might produce. The Mississippi became the nation's western boundary when the peace treaty was signed, but Spain controlled both banks along its lower reaches. Kentuckians and other westerners needed free navigation of the river and the right to deposit goods at New Orleans or some other suitable port for transshipment with little or no tax. Surpluses did not become a problem until 1784. Then, on June 26, 1784, Spanish officials closed the river to American traffic. Alarmed and infuriated by the action, Kentuckians were outraged when they learned of the attitude of the national government. In 1785-1786 John Jay, a New Yorker who was secretary of foreign affairs for the Articles of Confederation Congress, attempted to negotiate a comprehensive treaty with Don Diego Gardoqui, the Spanish representative to the United States. When Jay saw that Spain was adamantly opposed to American use of the Mississippi, he proposed that the United States waive its right to use of the river for twenty-five or thirty years in return for a satisfactory trade treaty. Jay believed there would be little American need to use the river during that period. Since nine votes were required to accept the treaty, Virginia and the other southern states were able to block it.[33] To westerners, Jay became a symbol of the hostile attitude of the northeastern states toward the West. Callous to western needs, would they block any effort to add Kentucky to the Union as a state? If they did so, should Kentucky look elsewhere for a solution to its most vital need? The injection of the Mississippi question with all of its ramifications made the separation issue in Kentucky even more complex.

TWO

The Early Conventions

Prior to 1784 the occasional demands for separation from Virginia had been overshadowed by the tribulations of the war years. By 1784 the peace treaty had been ratified and Kentucky's population was increasing rapidly. Although large scale Indian raids had almost ceased, an Indian scare in that year led to a meeting that resulted in the first of ten conventions, the last of which drafted a state constitution in 1792. Pioneer Benjamin Logan was the key figure in calling the initial meeting.

Logan established his station in Kentucky in 1775 when he was thirty-two years old. He brought out his family the next year, and his son William was the first white male born in Kentucky. A powerful six-foot, 180-pound man, Benjamin was noted for his strength and his skill in rough-and-tumble fighting. Described as straightforward, fearless, and prudent and a sage advisor, Logan led by example. He inspired confidence, although occasionally he was somewhat arbitrary and overbearing. During the war years he was at least Boone's equal as a pioneer leader. Logan helped block Henderson's Kentucky aspirations, and after the formation of Lincoln County he could have had any local office he wanted.[1] He was one of the few pioneer leaders who continued active participation in public affairs during the convention era and the early years of statehood. In the 1792 constitutional convention Logan was one of the few links with the recent past; he "represented those who

had fought and bled to make the new country safe as a home
for those who followed him."[2]

In the fall of 1784 Logan was colonel of the Lincoln County
militia. When he heard rumors of impending attacks by the
Cherokees and Chickamaugas from the south and other hostile
tribes from across the Ohio River, he called a meeting in
Danville to consider means of countering the danger. The district court was in session there and the meeting was well
attended. After Logan related what he had heard about the
Indians' hostile intent, Colonel William Fleming was installed
as chairman to direct the discussion. The following day Fleming was able to shift the presiding duties to Colonel Isaac
Shelby. Those present generally agreed that Kentucky's best
defense would be an expedition against the Indians in their
homeland. Caleb Wallace, George Muter, and a few others
protested that such action would be illegal since no one in
Kentucky had the authority to order an expedition outside the
limits of the District. If it was conducted without permission,
they warned, Virginia would probably refuse to pay its costs.
Ebenezer Brooks, who described himself as "an obscure little
man," defended the proposed action as necessary to preserve
law and order in the community. He insisted that volunteers
proceed with the expedition and that the governor be informed
why it was necessary. A motion to proceed passed unanimously. Brooks then proposed that they consider separation
from Virginia; the state constitution provided for such action,
and the Indian problem showed the need for it.[3]

Brooks's motion died without being seconded, and before
the end of the second day's deliberations Logan learned that
the Indian rumors were false. The men agreed, however, that
something should be done to provide for the common defense
when the menace was real. In a circular letter addressed to the
people they explained their concern and asked each militia
company to send a delegate to a meeting set for December 27,
1784, in Danville.[4] If the voting was in fact confined to members of the militia, some overaged or otherwise disqualified
men could not participate, but "militia company" may have
been used to designate voting areas. The great majority of men

in the District of Kentucky at that time were in the militia. One historian of the pioneer era, R.S. Cotterill, believed that the militia officers had already decided to seek autonomy and used the Indian scare as an excuse for initiating the separation movement.[5]

During the years between the December 1784 convention and the achievement of statehood on June 1, 1792, some Kentuckians lavished a great deal of time and attention upon the separation issue. Yet the struggle often involved a relatively small number of Kentucky's inhabitants. Unless stirred by some unusual event such as the closing of the Mississippi River to American traffic or a successful Indian raid, most Kentuckians were more interested in making a living than in debating political changes. The absence of regular political parties that could have formulated policies and positions and rallied support for them helps explain the usual public apathy over Kentucky's future. "I do not recall that there were any party divisions in the State at that time," James Taylor said in his autobiography, "except as to whether the seat of Government should be on the North or South side of the Kentucky River."[6]

Taylor was not altogether correct in his assertion. While parties did not exist in anything like their modern form, factions did form in Kentucky during the pre-statehood years. They were amorphous associations in a fluid political situation; they changed positions so frequently that it is difficult to ascertain precisely their goals and principles. Tenuous connections can sometimes be traced between them and the political parties that developed in the 1790s, but such trails should be followed with great caution.

Patricia Watlington, the historian who has made the most detailed study of the politics of this period, insists that three parties (not factions) existed.[7] The partisans were often considered "rabble" by their rivals. Although there were exceptions, the partisans were most often the landless men who came to Kentucky too late to get free land and were too poor to purchase good land. Since they had little hope of help from the Virginia government, they looked toward the national government for succor. If the Articles of Confederation Congress assumed jurisdiction over the western lands, the large Virginia grants might be rescinded and the land divided on a more equitable basis. When Kentucky became a state the partisans hoped to govern it on democratic principles that seemed radical to their opponents. They advocated statehood for Kentucky as long as that approach offered the possibility of redistributing the Virginia land grants; they opposed statehood after the mid-1780s when Congress accepted Virginia's requirement that Kentucky honor the Virginia grants. The partisans realized that the growing class of gentry might dominate a new government, and they feared that higher taxes would accompany this situation; statehood might jeopardize even the modest status they had acquired. Ebenezer Brooks, John Campbell, and Samuel Taylor, the best known partisan leaders, did not match up well with the leaders of the other two factions. In an effort to influence decisions they used county committees that attempted with little success to instruct the delegates to the Kentucky conventions. Unrestricted use of the Mississippi was vital to the sale of the crops they hoped to raise, and the partisans reacted violently to any threat to that economic lifeline. Strongest in the first of the ten conventions, the partisans also displayed considerable strength in the eighth and ninth conventions.

The gentry, sensitive to any threat to what they already possessed and to what they hoped to attain, were a small minority of the total population. They could not afford an arrogant, aristocratic stance that would alienate the mass of the people. Instead, they stressed the advantages of rule by a natural aristocracy through the election of enlightened men; the voters were assured that the ultimate political power was theirs. Fortified by a Burkesian concept of representation, the gentry rejected local attempts to instruct the delegates to the conventions. On the whole better educated than their partisan opponents, often related or associated through the extensive family ties for which Virginia was famous, the gentry might have been expected to maintain a tight unity against the more numerous partisans. Instead, they divided into two groups, a court faction and a country faction, which often fought each other. To a considerable degree the split resulted from and was sustained by personal and family animosities.

Definite boundaries cannot be drawn between the two factions of the Kentucky gentry. Members of the country faction were often called surveyors or planters. Most of them owned extensive acreages, often acquired through the generous fees in land collected by surveyors, and they were determined to retain what they had. They gave strong support to the new national government that might help protect property rights, and they opposed any effort to break away from it. While they saw the need for free access to the Mississippi River and an outlet port, they were perhaps more interested in opening trade routes with the eastern states. Their goals were often similar to those of the court faction, and the groups were often in substantial agreement. The Marshall family was the nucleus of the country faction. Colonel Thomas Marshall, father of the future chief justice of the United States, was the leader of the clan, but nephew Humphrey Marshall was the best hater. Humphrey had the ability to enrage opponents, at times to the dueling stage, and his frequent controversies enlivened Kentucky politics for several decades. He had the last word in most of his encounters, for in 1812 he published the first comprehensive history of Kentucky, and it was less than objective in describing his many quarrels. Other country leaders included Robert Bullitt, Robert Breckinridge, John Edwards, Joseph Crockett, and, some of the time, George Muter. This faction wanted an amiable separation from Virginia upon mutually agreeable terms, followed by admission into the Union.

Lawyers and judges were the core of the court faction. Its membership grew in the 1780s as more courts were created in Kentucky and more lawyers rushed in to share the profits from the endless land cases. Well educated by contemporary standards, they were accustomed to being in the public eye, and they were trained in oral and written communications. Their ambitions usually included the acquisition of land, for that remained one of the tests of a gentleman, but most of them arrived in Kentucky too late to acquire the large tracts they desired. Their estates usually depended upon purchase, including the acres often accepted in lieu of money fees. The court men were intensely interested in the political structure of which they were a part, and they dominated several of the conventions held in the 1780s. Economic development was also one of their strong interests.

The court faction was the group most likely to promote manufacturing and commerce, and use of the Mississippi was vital to their economic dreams. Although the Jay-Gardoqui Treaty, which would have denied Americans use of the river for an extended period, was rejected in Congress, the margin of defeat was a matter of concern. The court men began to wonder if the eastern states, particularly those in the northeast, had a genuine concern for western problems. Some even doubted the degree of Virginia's concern for its citizens on the western waters. Perhaps Kentucky should declare independence from the Old Dominion without negotiating an agreement. Then Kentucky could select the most promising option. It could be statehood if the United States offered favorable terms; it could be continued independence, aided by an association with Great Britain or Spain; it could be incorporation on favorable terms into the Spanish empire. James Wilkinson, one of the most accomplished intriguers in American history, assumed the leadership of this faction. Their subsequent involvement with the "Spanish Conspiracy" complicated the separation movement, tainted the reputations of some prominent individuals, and enlivened Kentucky politics and historical writing far into the future. Among the other leaders were John Fowler, Benjamin Sebastian, John Brown, Harry Innes, Caleb Wallace, Samuel McDowell and George Muter, although the last later switched to their country rivals.

By the end of 1784 Kentucky's population was estimated at 30,000 and was increasing rapidly. Indian depredations continued to be a problem although the large British-directed raids had ceased. District Attorney Walker Daniel warned Governor Benjamin Harrison in May that the government's failure "to prevent the cruelties & Depredations of the Savages" was leading the settlers to "wish for a separation, because they then expect that every one in power will be equally interested with themselves in securing a friendly Intercourse with their troublesome Neighbors." (Three months later Indians killed Daniel.) Conditions gradually improved, and in early 1784 Levi Todd reported that "the People who have been confined to Forts are now entering the Woods, beginning the World, Stately Houses in a few years will be reared where small Log Cabbins have Stood, Wheat Fields & Meadows where Cane Brakes now grow."[8] Future prospects seemed limitless if a sympathetic government would finally end the Indian menace. Paradoxically, as the major Indian danger decreased, the settlers seemed to be equally upset by the much smaller raids that continued. Indian attacks were expected during the Revolutionary War; they should not be tolerated in a rapidly growing, peacetime community.

After Logan's November meeting, most militia companies selected a delegate as instructed, and a majority of those elected were in Danville on Monday, December 27, 1784. That village was one of Kentucky's newest communities. When a court was created for the District of Kentucky in March 1783, Harrodsburg, which had been the informal political center for the region, had no facility adequate to house it. The court appointed its clerk, John May, and District Attorney Daniel to select a site for the construction of a courthouse and jail near John Crow's Station. Soon known as Danville, the village was in effect the capital of the District until statehood was attained.[9]

Thirty delegates were present on December 27: nine from Jefferson County, seven from Fayette, fourteen from Lincoln. William Fleming of Lincoln County was elected president, and Thomas Perkins, a nonmember, was appointed clerk. Three members were appointed to examine credentials, and the convention adjourned until they could report. The next morning the committee reported favorably on thirty-two delegates, although James Rogers of Jefferson County was still absent; William Moore (Lincoln) had presented his credentials that

morning before the committee reported. Later in the day
Squire Boone, Samuel McDowell, and Christopher Irvine arrived and were seated. As far as factional affiliation can be
determined, the partisans seem to have had a majority. The
best known members, or the ones who would become well
known during the next several years, were Christopher Greenup, Caleb Wallace, Ebenezer Brooks, Samuel McDowell, and
William Fleming. Unfortunately there was no James Madison
to take careful notes on the discussions and debates. The journal provides only a sketchy summary of official actions, with
no effort to record what was said.[10]

Since the convention had not been authorized by any official or agency of the state, the delegates decided to justify
their meeting. They adopted unanimously two resolutions:
"That the Inhabitants of this District have a right peacably to
Assemble to consider their Greevances and adopt such Measures as they shall think prudent for redress," and "That the said
Inhabitants are intitled to equal Liberty and Privileges with
their Brethren in the Eastern part of this State." Then they
decided to discuss on Wednesday in committee-of-the-whole
"Whether Laws which from their nature impose Taxes on the
Inhabitants of the Western Waters only, whether expressly, or
from their operation are greevous and against the fundamen-
tal rights of the People." This protest was aimed at a recent tax
of five shillings per 100 acres on future land grants that exceeded 1,400 acres, with certain exceptions. It was much more
likely to be applied in western than in eastern Virginia, and the
Kentuckians who hoped to acquire extensive estates were adamantly opposed to it.[11]

Benjamin Logan and Isaac Shelby, two of the West's most
noted pioneers, arrived and took their seats on Wednesday,
December 29. Shelby was made chairman of the committee-of-
the-whole when it met to consider the state of the District. He
later reported that the committee had not had time to consider
the second grievance referred to it. His recommendation that it
be referred to a select committee was adopted.

Latecomer Samuel Scott arrived on Thursday, December
30, before Caleb Wallace reported for the select committee. He

introduced a series of resolutions, listing thirteen grievances, that were read twice and adopted by the convention. The first resolution, presumably the most urgent, dealt with Kentucky's legal inability to take offensive action against the hostile tribes. The delegates were so critical of what they considered excessive court delays that they called the district judges to appear before the committee-of-the-whole to justify the slowness of their procedure. They also objected to the District's Supreme Court being supported by the fines it collected instead of general appropriations, and to one-sixth of the surveyors' fees going to support the College of William and Mary instead of the local Transylvania Seminary. On land issues the delegates registered their protest against "the practice of Surveyors in Surveying the same Tract of Land for sundry Persons . . . because it tends to multiply litigations and Subjects the Claimants to unnecessary expense." They also complained because the registrar demanded his fees "for issuing a Grant to Lands before the same is obtained," and they called for "the Introduction of a Printer into the District" so the people could be informed of what was happening. They requested assistance for orphans and the poor, equitable laws for the improvement of the breeds of horses, and realistic regulations for the reporting of stray animals. Shelby presided again when the convention went into committee-of-the-whole, then asked and received permission for it to meet again to complete its deliberations. Before adjournment, a select committee was appointed to correct the minutes.[12]

The convention assembled at ten o'clock on the last morning of the year and again turned itself into a committee. Later that day Shelby sought and received permission for the committee-of-the-whole to continue discussion the following day. The convention lost a member when Joseph Barnett was granted a leave of absence to return to Jefferson County. Work continued in committee on New Year's Day 1785, and the convention accepted several corrections in its minutes. No session was held on Sunday, and on Monday, January 3, the members decided to postpone the order of the day to Tuesday.[13]

The Tuesday session was a busy one. Shelby presented a series of resolutions recommended by the committee-of-the-whole, most of which were read and adopted without serious dissent. The only recorded vote of the entire convention came on the second resolution that objected to the five-shilling land tax "Because it is partial in its operation and in many instances a retrospective Law." The resolution passed, 12-9, with many of the delegates abstaining. The "Yeas" were Richard C. Anderson, John Campbell, Isaac Morrison, Isaac Cox, Philip Philips, Andrew Hinds, John Edward King, Christopher Greenup, James Harrod, Isaac Hite, Ebenezer Brooks, and Willis Green; the first seven were all from Jefferson County. The "Nays" were William Kincheloe, John Logan, William Kennedy, Caleb Wallace, Robert Moseby, William Moore, Isaac Shelby, Samuel McDowell, and Benjamin Logan; most of them represented Lincoln County.

The convention then heard and accepted as satisfactory an explanation of court delays from Samuel McDowell and Caleb Wallace, two convention delegates who were also members of the District's Supreme Court. They explained that two judges had been killed by Indians and a third had refused the appointment. Furthermore, the court had not received a legal copy of the records of the Court of Commissions, and the court's funding was so inadequate that necessary facilities and supplies were often unavailable. As a result, a "fair tryal & Just decision could seldome be obtained whilst the Court is destitute of the conveniences we have enumerated." [14]

Several other protests were also approved. The convention denounced unfair taxes; duties should not be charged on goods coming down the Ohio River; judges should be paid from state funds, not from fees; land grants should not be larger than was needed to support a family; nonresidents should not be appointed to positions in the District. Most if not all of these grievances could be remedied by the state or national government. But there were others caused by "the remote Situation of the District from the seat of Government" that "can not be redressed whilst it remains a part of Virginia." This group of grievances protested against the expense of legal appeals to

Richmond; the lack of a District legislature to check executive officers; a pardoning power in the District for death penalties that was said to conflict with the state constitution; the delay in learning of new laws; and the drainage eastward of money.[15] Approval of these complaints clearly pointed to the advantages to be derived by separation from Virginia. But that issue had not been put to the voters when they had elected the delegates, and most of the convention members who favored separation did not believe they could provide for it without a mandate to that effect from their constituents.

Without a roll call vote, the convention voted to call another convention to meet in May 1785 "to take the Expediency of the proposed Seperation into consideration as also the several grievances stated by this Convention and to adopt such measures there upon and whatever else may come before them, as they may Judge most conducive to the Interests of the District." The convention then made a radical departure from the Virginia practice of electing delegates or representatives on the basis of county equality. Believing that "in the choise of the proposed Convention the People should have as equal a representation according to their numbers as conveniently can be obtained," the delegates voted to allocate the twenty-eight seats among the counties according to their estimated population. Fayette and Jefferson counties were given eight seats; Lincoln got twelve. Jefferson and Lincoln were divided into election districts. In an effort to get a more accurate population count, the delegates were requested to take a census in their districts before the next convention convened.[16]

Before adjourning on Wednesday, January 5, the convention voted to send a copy of its proceedings to the commanding officer in each county so that the people might know what had been done. The records were ordered lodged with Willis Green of Lincoln County for safekeeping and the use of the next convention, which was to assemble on the fourth Monday in May, court day in Danville. A gentleman spectator who had attended sessions of the convention commented favorably on its "style of moderation," although "several spirited propositions were discussed." Easterners could not call it a meeting of "rabble," he declared, for "several very able men were members."[17]

By the time of adjournment, some members of the court faction had come to favor severance from Virginia, as the partisans had for some time. The country faction continued to favor the Virginia connection, although it hoped for improvements in the relationship that would benefit Kentucky. While the partisan and court factions were becoming more united in seeking separation, they disagreed on how to obtain it and what should be done when it was won. If the partisans could not secure separation through Congressional action, most of them were willing to declare independence without seeking Virginia's consent. Once a state was formed, they would redistribute the large land grants. But this threat was becoming less important by 1785 as a number of partisans had managed to obtain land. The court faction adhered to the idea of a parting based on an agreement negotiated with the Virginia government. An essential item in the agreement would be the sanctity of land titles. This group's switch to a separation policy may have been based in part on its members' desire to control affairs in Kentucky. They saw themselves as the logical officeholders in the new state. While factional allegiance is difficult to ascertain in the absence of organized parties, roll call votes, and detailed reporting, the partisans appear to have had more members in the first convention than the court faction. The surveyors may have had only two.[18]

The second convention began with a dispute over its membership. John Campbell, a Jefferson County partisan who had served in the first convention, believed that the redistribution of seats ordered for the May meeting was a plot by the Fayette and Lincoln County members to dominate the proceedings. Following his leadership, the Jefferson County partisans elected twelve delegates instead of the eight allocated to the county. In addition, Nelson County, recently formed from Jefferson, also elected twelve delegates although not authorized to have any.

But on May 23, the scheduled opening day, only the Fayette

and Lincoln County delegates were in Danville. Without waiting for the others to arrive, they elected Samuel McDowell president, made Thomas Todd clerk, and proceeded with other business. Four days later, Campbell and fourteen of the missing delegates appeared and demanded that everything that had been done before their arrival be rescinded. Their demand was rejected, and an explosive confrontation seemed certain. But a compromise was reached when the opposing groups discovered that they were in general agreement on separation. The actions taken during the first few days were allowed to stand, and the tardy irregular delegates were seated without scrutiny of their dubious credentials. When Campbell refused to accept the compromise and went home in a pout, Brooks was left as the partisan leader. Control of this convention had shifted to the court faction. With McDowell in the chair, Innes, Wallace, Muter, and Logan were the key members.

After the danger of a clash was averted, the convention moved "with great caution and equal moderation" to a unanimous decision on May 31 to petition the General Assembly for separation. The petition repeated the now-familiar reasons for severance but emphasized that Kentucky wanted "the most perfect harmony with our brethren in other parts of the state." The delegates asserted that they would draft a constitution and seek admission into the Union as soon as possible. The proposed state was to be named the Commonwealth of Kentucky, and Virginia laws would remain in effect until and unless changed. A question to be resolved was how much of the state debt Kentucky would assume.

The petition was not forwarded to the Virginia General Assembly. Some of the delegates with sensitive constitutional scruples may have remained troubled by the irregular election of a substantial number of their membership; others apparently wanted absolute assurance, before taking definite action, that their decision represented the will of the people. To the dismay of members who believed that separation was long overdue, the convention voted to withhold the petition and to call yet another convention to meet in Danville on the second Monday in August 1785. Representation would again be based on population estimates rather than county equality. Lincoln County was assigned ten delegates, Fayette eight, and Jefferson and Nelson six each. Humphrey Marshall was convinced that this approach was designed to win popular support for the break with Virginia.[19]

To explain their position, the convention issued "An Address to the Inhabitants of the District of Kentucky." Its florid style suggested that James Wilkinson was its author, although illness had prevented his attending the convention. Since the District still lacked a press, copies were sent to the counties for posting on courthouse doors. The author patterned the Address after the Declaration of Independence: "In every case where it becomes necessary for one part of the community to separate from the other, duty to Almighty God, and a decent respect for the opinions of mankind, require that the causes which impel them thereto, should be clearly and impartially set forth." When a government failed to provide "the ease and protection" for which it was formed, "it is the right, it is the duty of the people, to seek such other mode, as will be most likely to ensure to themselves and their posterity those blessings to which by nature they are entitled." The Address listed the familiar charges against the Virginia relationship: no authority to use the militia effectively against the Indians; no executive in the District to enforce laws or grant pardons; continued ignorance of recently enacted laws; inadequate protection; an unfavorable balance of trade. Because of its remote distance from the seat of government, the Address charged, Kentuckians would never derive equal benefits from the Virginia government, and the District's commercial interests were distinctly different from those of eastern Virginia. Because of these considerations, the convention had decided to request separation from Virginia followed by admission to the Union as an independent state. The Address admitted that some doubters wondered if the District could fill the offices of the proposed government with qualified people and if the inhabitants of the new state could adequately support it. The answer to both questions, the Address declared, was yes.[20]

Caleb Wallace, a Presbyterian minister-lawyer-judge, had

James Wilkinson (1757-1825) had a career filled with intrigues, all of which he survived. *Courtesy of The Filson Club, Louisville.*

been appointed to the Supreme Court of Kentucky in August 1783 after John Floyd was killed by Indians. Wallace corresponded frequently with James Madison, who had been a class behind him at Princeton. By the close of the second convention Wallace was convinced that "it was better to part in peace than to remain together in a State of Jealousy and Discontent." Having decided "that our Situation is too remote to enjoy the advantages of Government with Virginia in any tolerable degree," he worried if "we shall lack wisdom and virtue to govern ourselves." As a partial answer to those concerns he asked Madison to prepare a form of government that he would like to live under if he were a Kentuckian. Wallace included specific questions that would have to be answered in framing a constitution: the best form of representation; terms and conditions of officeholding; periodic review of the constitution; and the proper relationships among the branches of government.[21] Wallace obviously believed that a constitution would be required within the near future.

Thirty members were apparently elected to the third convention, which met in Danville on August 8, 1785, although only twenty-six were listed as attending. McDowell was again elected to preside and Todd continued as clerk. Partisan leaders John Campbell and Ebenezer Brooks were absent, and the court faction dominated the session. Most important among the new members were James Wilkinson and Benjamin Sebastian; both would have important roles from this time on. Once again, most of the work was done in committee-of-the-whole, with George Muter presiding. This committee reworked and modified the undelivered petition from the last convention, then reported a series of resolutions that were adopted unanimously. This convention's major premise was "that the situation of this district, upwards of five hundred miles from the seat of the present government, with the intervention of a mountainous desert of two hundred miles passed only at particular seasons, and never without danger from hostile nations of savages, precludes every idea of a connection on republican principles, and originates many grievances." The familiar litany of grievances was repeated, along with a condemnation of the five-shilling land tax that was called as "equally subversive of justice as any of the statutes of the British parliament, that impelled the good people of America to arms."

Then came the decisive resolution to which all members of the convention had agreed: "That it is the indispensable duty of this convention, as they regard the prosperity and happiness of their constituents, themselves, and posterity, to make application to the General Assembly, at the ensuing session, for an act to separate this district from the present government forever, on terms honourable to both and injurious to neither; in order that it may enjoy all the advantages, privileges, and amenities of a free, sovereign and independent republic." To expedite this request, the convention decided to have George Muter, the chief justice of the District, and Harry Innes, the district attorney, carry it to the General Assembly and lobby for its acceptance. The convention did not provide for a constitutional convention; when Virginia gave her anticipated consent to separation, the act would presumably provide for one.[22] At this point none of the three conventions had addressed the national government under the Articles of Confederation.

Before adjourning, the delegates adopted two addresses, one to the General Assembly, the other "To the Inhabitants of the District of Kentucky." James Wilkinson probably drafted both documents. His selection for the tasks was a tribute to the abilities and personality of a newcomer who had lived in Kentucky only since February 1784. For almost a decade he was easily the most important politician in Kentucky. Born in Maryland in 1757, Wilkinson rose to the rank of brigadier general during the American Revolution. He also displayed a talent for intrigue. Associated with the Conway Cabal, which reportedly sought to replace George Washington as commander-in-chief, Wilkinson disengaged in time to save his army career. He became the army's clothier-general, but irregularities in his accounts led to his resignation in March 1781 before official action could be taken against him. Various agricultural and commercial ventures in Pennsylvania did not produce the income needed to satisfy his expensive tastes, so

Wilkinson turned to Kentucky, where men of ability and ambition were said to prosper. Associated with Philadelphia mercantile interests, he opened Lexington's first store in 1784 and was soon seeking profits in a number of enterprises, including land speculation.

Humphrey Marshall, who became Wilkinson's most implacable Kentucky foe, described the man he detested with surprising objectivity. "A person, not quite tall enough to be perfectly elegant, was compensated by its symmetry, and appearance of health, and strength. A countenance, open, capacious, mild, and beaming with intelligence; a gait, firm, manly, and facile; manners, bland, accommodating, and popular; an address, easy, polite and gracious; invited approach, gave access, assured attention, cordiality, and ease. By these fair forms he conciliated; by these, he captivated." These were first impressions, Marshall warned; they would be modified upon closer acquaintance.[23] Wilkinson's florid style of speech and writing was much admired in that era, and he was fluent with tongue and pen. Noted for his lavish hospitality, he had particular appeal to young men, who were attracted by his openhandedness and his air of sophistication. His expensive lifestyle put Wilkinson in constant need of money to cover his many debts. Egotistical, ambitious, and self-confident, Wilkinson often referred to the code of honor by which he professed to live. It was flexible enough to sanctify actions for him that to others might appear deceitful, unscrupulous, dishonest, and treasonable. Within a few years, before Kentucky attained statehood, Wilkinson would become associated with a "Spanish Conspiracy" that tainted his reputation and those of several men who were unfortunate enough to be associated with him. But in 1785 the Spanish association had not been made, and Wilkinson showed promise of assuming the leadership of Kentucky in the statehood movement.

"To the Inhabitants of the District of Kentucky" described in exaggerated terms the Indian danger and called upon the people to abandon the lethargy and supineness that might soon result in their being "huddled together in stations; a situation in our present circumstances, scarcely preferable to

Humphrey Marshall (1706-1841), Wilkinson's most implacable Kentucky foe, wrote the state's first general history. *Courtesy of The Filson Club, Louisville.*

death." The county lieutenants were urged to improve the preparedness of the militia and to "concert such plans as they may deem expedient for the defense of our country, or for carrying expeditions against the hostile nations of Indians."[24] This proposal hinted that action might be taken without regard to the Virginia laws and policies regarding Indian affairs.

The address to the General Assembly carried traces of belligerency in its blunt approach. "In this address," it warned, "we have discarded the complimentary style of adulation and insincerity. It becomes freemen when speaking to freemen, to employ the plain, manly, unadorned language of independence, supported by conscious rectitude." After repeating the reasons for seeking separation, the address suggested that it would be unique in world history for "a sovereign power solely intent to bless its people, agreeing to the dismemberment of its parts, in order to serve the happiness of the whole." The request was almost a demand: "We, therefore, with the consent, and by the authority of our constituents, after the most solemn deliberation, being warned of every consequence which can ensure, for them, for ourselves, and for posterity unborn—do pray that an act may pass at the ensuing session of assembly, declaring and acknowledging the sovereignty and independence of this district."[25]

While the request did not include subsequent admission to the Union, that step was generally assumed to be certain. While blunt, the request was clearly within constitutional bounds, and opposition to it was minimal. Caleb Wallace in a letter to James Madison was one of the few Kentuckians who left a written protest, and his concern was more with the style of the request than with its aim. He was "not pleased with the Splendid Dress" of the document; he wished that the substance of the resolutions passed by the convention had made up the body of the address. Wallace hoped that "the impropriety in form will not injure a Cause which I am anxious should be determined on the most friendly and liberal principles."[26]

James Monroe, the future president, was one of the eastern Virginians who openly opposed separation, although he was

This replica of the Mercer County Courthouse in which most of the ten conventions met was built on Constitution Square, Danville, in 1942. Spectators found little space in the crowded room. *Courtesy of the Kentucky Department of Parks.*

Benjamin Grayson's tavern, built in 1785 near the courthouse, housed many of the delegates to the conventions. *Courtesy of the Kentucky Department of Parks.*

resigned to its success. He believed that the state could answer the complaints of the West by making some changes in the government. His major objection to the detachment was that it would diminish the status and power of Virginia in the national government. Monroe even suggested that the Atlantic states should curb the growth of the West lest at some future date the western states might outnumber the eastern ones. Once the West secured the use of the Mississippi River, Monroe warned, they would lose interest in eastern affairs. During a trip to Kentucky in 1785 he expressed his opposition to separation, but he made little impression upon such leaders as Sam McDowell. Monroe's objections were considered to be of little consequence.[27]

Muter and Innes had little difficulty in securing an Enabling Act from the Virginia General Assembly. James Madison, a member of the Virginia House, apparently drafted the measure that the House approved on January 6, 1786. John Brown, senator from the District of Kentucky, was a member of the Senate committee that recommended passage in the upper house. The Virginia Senate approved the bill on January 10, and it was signed on January 16. Kentuckians found several grounds for complaint in the terms imposed by the act, the most common complaint being another delay before separation could be completed.

Instead of providing for a constitutional convention, the act required that another convention gather in Danville on the fourth Monday in September 1786. Each of the seven counties would send five delegates, elected at the August court days in the same fashion as the members of the General Assembly. The convention was charged to determine whether it was "the will of the good people of the said district" to become an independent state upon the terms contained in the act:

1. The boundary of Virginia would remain the same as the existing district boundary.

2. Kentucky would assume a just proportion of Virginia's public debt.

3. The Virginia land grants would remain valid and secure.

4. Kentucky would not tax the lands of nonresidents at a

higher rate than was paid by residents, and for six years non-resident lands could not be subject to forfeiture or other penalty for neglect of cultivation or other improvements.

5. Previously issued land warrants could continue to be located in Kentucky until September 1, 1788.

6. The Kentucky lands set aside for military and other services would remain at Virginia's disposal until September 1, 1788, after which the unclaimed land would revert to Kentucky.

7. Use of the Ohio River would be free for all citizens of the United States.

8. Disputes over the terms of separation would be settled by six commissioners, two of them appointed by each party and the other two selected by the first four.

If the September 1786 convention accepted the terms, it would set a day "posterior" to September 1, 1787, on which independence would become effective. Prior to June 1, 1787, however, the Congress of the United States would have to agree to admit the new state to the Union and to release Virginia from all federal obligations in regard to Kentucky. To prevent "a period of anarchy," the September 1786 convention was authorized to call a constitutional convention before June 1, 1787, and to determine what Virginia laws would remain in effect until the new state's legislature could act on them.[28]

These requirements caused considerable dismay and irritation in Kentucky. The people had already expressed their desire for statehood; why was another convention necessary? Since Kentucky had received so few benefits from Virginia, why should it have to assume any part of the state debt? Why should a sovereign state not have complete control of its lands? Why could admission to the Union not be negotiated after statehood was obtained? Did Kentucky not have the right to determine access to a river that flowed through its territory? (Madison reminded Muter that Kentucky could hardly object to free use of the Ohio since that was the right she claimed for the Mississippi.)[29]

The Kentucky reaction to the Enabling Act led to some realignment of the major political factions. The court faction, unhappy with some of the restrictions in the act, began to talk of unilateral separation without regard to the procedure and time schedule mandated by Virginia. James Wilkinson became the most vocal advocate of this approach. The country faction was most closely associated with land laws and policies. Since the Enabling Act fully protected their Virginia titles, they strongly supported separation on the terms in the act. Some of the partisans who had favored immediate severance began to advocate delay; they believed that Kentucky needed Virginia's support in securing free use of the Mississippi, and they feared it would not be available once Kentucky was independent. Samuel Taylor of Lincoln County even circulated a petition requesting the next convention to delay following the pre-scribed road to statehood. Some of the partisans were begin-ning to realize that their opponents would never accept a redistribution of large land holdings; their goals would have to be more realistic.[30] In the absence of party organizations and platforms, some interesting ad hoc combinations were formed during the next several years.

James Wilkinson led the opposition to the Enabling Act, and the August voting for delegates created more excitement than had been present in the earlier elections. As a candidate for one of the five Fayette County seats, Wilkinson delivered a fiery three-and-a-half hour speech on the first day of the five-day election period. During his call for immediate separation Wilkinson made an unfortunate slip when he insisted that "posterior to September 1, 1787" in the Enabling Act meant before that date, not after it. A rival candidate, twenty-six-year-old Humphrey Marshall, pounced upon the error. A conserva-tive lawyer who later became a leading Federalist in the state, Marshall scored heavily when he taunted Wilkinson for his misuse of the word. "Either he did not know the meaning of the word, 'posterior'; or meant to impose on his audience. That, in the one case, he was unfit to guide—in the other, unsafe to follow."

Marshall believed that he lost the election because of trick-ery. When voting on the first day ran against Wilkinson and his friends, Marshall declared, the sheriff closed the polls early and most of Marshall's rural supporters went home, but they intended to return and vote on the final day. But militia officers who favored Wilkinson ordered militia musters in the county on the fifth day, and many of Marshall's voters were unable to vote. Marshall's dislike of Wilkinson became an obsessive hatred.[31]

The delegates who were in Danville on September 26, 1786, were not able to form a quorum. Persistent Indian raids in 1785-1786 persuaded Virginia Governor Patrick Henry to recall George Rogers Clark from retirement to lead an expedition against the Wabash tribes while Benjamin Logan attacked the Shawnee in their homeland. While the expeditions were less successful than had been hoped for, they pressured the Indians into negotiations that led to a peace settlement in the spring of 1787. Meanwhile, the campaigns kept a number of convention delegates from Danville. Those in Danville adjourned from day to day while waiting for their colleagues to return. Without legal authority to do so, they sent a memorial to the General Assembly in which they explained the delay and asked for several changes in the Enabling Act. John Marshall, the future chief justice of the United States, was made the agent to push Kentucky's cause in Richmond.[32]

With the convention in abeyance, some of the idle delegates turned to the Danville Political Club as a forum for discussing economic and political issues. Organized in late December 1786, its members included such politically active Kentuckians as Harry Innes, Christopher Greenup, Thomas Todd, George Muter, Peyton Short, Samuel McDowell, and Benjamin Sebastian. "It was a training school for the future statesmen of Kentucky," a historian later wrote, and their discussions included most of the important issues confronting the westerners. In a typical meeting, two prepared members discussed the assigned topic in some detail; when they concluded, the floor was open for general and often spirited discussion. Major Erkuries Beatty, an army paymaster who visited Danville in April 1787, complained in his diary: "Very much disturbed by a Political Club which met in the next room where we slept and kept us awake until 12 or 1 o'clock."

Members of the club became excited over such topics as separation from Virginia, the advantages of a one- or two-house legislature, the Enabling Act, use of the Mississippi River, the cultivation of tobacco, intermarriage with Indians, the essential features of a constitution, and a four-meeting detailed analysis of the new federal constitution. The Political Club remained active until at least 1790, and its debates must have been of considerable value to its members who also served in some of the ten conventions.[33]

Sometime in January 1787 a quorum was achieved as the moderately successful warriors returned to Kentucky. Because of the conditions Virginia had imposed, there was increased opposition to separation, but by a wide margin the delegates voted "that it was expedient for, and the will of the good people of the district to separate from the state of Virginia and become an independent state." All was going well; statehood was in sight. Then Samuel Taylor rode in from the East, bringing with him a Second Enabling Act, passed because "unforeseen events" had prevented the convention from meeting at the designated time and had made it impossible for the deadlines to be met. Kentuckians were believed to be so divided on the issue (probably because of the petitions from Taylor and other partisans) that another expression of opinion was needed.[34]

The Second Enabling Act told each county to elect five convention delegates at the August 1787 court days. The convention would meet in Danville on the third Monday in September. A quorum would consist of a majority of the whole membership. If two-thirds of the members had not appeared after fifteen days, a majority of those present would constitute a valid number for action. If the convention voted again for separation, it should fix a date not later than January 1, 1789, for final independence. It should also arrange for a constitutional convention. Separation was contingent upon Congress agreeing before July 4, 1788, to admit Kentucky to the Union and to release Virginia from all federal obligations regarding Kentucky. The act also directed Virginia's representatives in Congress "to use their endeavors to obtain from Congress a speedy concurrence in the measure proposed in this and the act heretofore passed."[35] This second act did not repeal the conditions set forth in the first one; it extended the time limits and required yet another vote for separation.

Many members of the fourth convention were angered by this enforced delay. Some of them wanted to ignore the new act and continue with their work, but the majority concluded that the Second Enabling Act had terminated their charge. Soon after the convention closed, George Muter learned from James Madison that the convention could have continued, but by then it was too late to reconvene.[36]

Dissatisfaction over the unexpected delay was exacerbated by news about the John Jay-Don Diego Gardoqui negotiations. Westerners bristled with indignation when they heard that Jay was willing to waive American rights to the use of the Mississippi River for a twenty-five or thirty-year period in return for a commercial treaty. Jay did not believe that the United States would have much need for use of the river until well beyond that period; Kentuckians knew that the need had already arrived and that each year would see the need grow as agricultural surpluses increased. The advocates of increased manufacturing foresaw an even greater role for river traffic in the future. Unrestricted use of the Mississippi was one issue on which almost all Kentuckians agreed.

Madison understood the West better than Jay did. Abandoning the use of the Mississippi, Madison wrote Thomas Jefferson, would indicate to the westerners that they were being sold out by the East. If it were done, Madison warned, the westerners might be justified in considering "themselves as absolved from every federal tie" and free to "court some protection for their betrayed rights." Several prominent Kentuckians, including Harry Innes, Benjamin Logan, and Samuel McDowell, became interested in Arthur Campbell's apparently successful effort to establish the independent state of Franklin in western North Carolina. An intriguing possibility at which Campbell hinted was a general unification of the western country.[37]

Soon after the end of the fourth convention, a Pittsburgh committee of correspondence asked for help in blocking the

Jay-Gardoqui treaty. On March 29, 1787, John Brown, Harry Innes, George Muter, and Benjamin Sebastian issued a circular letter in which they called for a special meeting to consider the hostile actions of Congress and to protest them. The four sponsors also suggested that committees of correspondence established throughout the West could coordinate the efforts of the protesters. A meeting was held in May, but it did little more than reemphasize the western distrust of the eastern government. Some of its members may have hoped to use this unofficial meeting as a springboard to immediate secession. That action could have been covered by a provision in the call for the meeting: "and to adopt such other measures as may be most conducive to our happiness." Those who shared that hope were disappointed. Tension eased when westerners realized that Virginia and other southern states would block the detested treaty in Congress. While a committee of correspondence was set up, a proposed remonstrance was rejected.[38] The results were so disappointing that this convention is not considered to be one of the ten that marked Kentucky's efforts to gain statehood.

The results might have been different had James Wilkinson been present to lead the movement. But while the May meeting frittered away its time, Wilkinson was on his way to New Orleans and the beginning of the "Spanish Conspiracy." He and it would soon further complicate the separation movement.

THREE

A Spanish Conspiracy?

James Wilkinson spent lavishly, both for himself and his family and for the extensive entertaining that was designed to impress others and thus help his political ambitions. But he had limited resources when he came to Kentucky, and his varied economic ventures failed to provide the income he needed. By the mid-1780s he was heavily in debt. Yet he was so convincing in his explanations and so plausible in his assurances that he managed to maintain his precarious status. Upon one occasion when an irate creditor came to demand repayment of a substantial sum, Wilkinson borrowed an additional amount before the bemused man departed.[1] That was at best an uncertain source of income, and Wilkinson never considered making a drastic cut in his heavy expenditures. What he wanted was a drastic increase in his income. In a daring and audacious attempt to restore his solvency he decided to secure from the Spanish authorities a monopoly on trade on the Mississippi River between Kentucky and the Spanish settlements on that stream.

By 1787 Kentucky was producing surpluses of several crops. The District's small urban population provided a very limited market, and the cost of sending produce overland to the eastern markets was prohibitive. The river outlet was the only feasible route to markets, but the Spanish authorities had closed it. In earlier years most of the limited trade had consisted of furs and deerskins; tobacco, flour, hams, bacon, and butter were now available for sale. But the occasional boat that tried to evade the embargo was seized and its cargo confiscated. Some Americans were allowed to immigrate into Spanish territory, but they were forbidden to bring goods for sale without paying a prohibitive duty. Still, there was a potentially lucrative market in the Spanish towns and an even better one if goods could be shipped from the New Orleans port. Always a gambler, Wilkinson decided to see if he could get the trade opened, preferably with a monopoly for him. A failure might ruin him, but if he succeeded he might win the wealth he longed for. In his desperate situation, the risk was acceptable.

Wilkinson left Kentucky in April 1787 with a flatboat laden with a cargo of tobacco, bacon, hams, and flour. Threatened with seizure at the Spanish ports along the river, he persuaded local officials to let him continue to New Orleans. The two fine horses he gave to an official at Natchez reinforced his oral arguments. Wilkinson delayed to make some visits on the way, and his cargo reached New Orleans before he did. When officials there started to impound the boat and its load they were warned off by merchants who were acquainted with Wilkinson, at least by correspondence. They were told that Wilkinson was very popular in Kentucky and that the seizure of his property might cause Kentuckians, already provoked by Spanish policy, to take military action on their own without regard for the official policy of the United States. Indeed, it was hinted, Wilkinson might have been sent to provoke an incident that would allow the United States to seize all of Louisiana. Governor Esteban Rodriguez Miro decided to move cautiously.[2]

After his arrival in New Orleans on July 2, 1787, Wilkinson soon ingratiated himself with officials. In conversations and then in a lengthy "First Memorial" that he wrote in early September for Miro to send to his government, he warned that elements in the United States wanted to take the Spanish lands by force. Kentucky, angered by the United States' willingness to waive its use of the Mississippi River, was near separation from the nation. Once independent, Wilkinson argued, Kentucky would have to seek help from some foreign power. He had been sent to New Orleans to ascertain the Spanish position should Kentucky become independent. Would Spain consider an association with Kentucky then? A wily negotiator, Wilkinson represented himself as a person with sufficient influence to direct events in Kentucky and to keep the wild backwoodsmen in check. He had prepared a basis for his claims and had effectively eliminated one person who might have challenged him by helping discredit George Rogers Clark with false reports on his activities and charges that he had become a drunkard. Wilkinson also claimed that he could promote the migration of Kentuckians into Spanish territory. Miro hoped to increase the number of immigrants by promising that Kentuckians who made the move would be able to retain their religion and their form of local government.

"The delivering up of Kentucky unto his Majesty's hands" was Wilkinson's primary object, Miro reported to his government. Since it would be at least several months before he could receive a reply from Spain, Miro gave Wilkinson permission to ship goods up to a value of $37,000 to New Orleans. The Kentuckian was not given a monopoly, but the permission had that effect since no other permits were issued.[3]

Wilkinson could hardly have asked for greater success. His finances were improved, with even greater possibilities for the future, his Kentucky popularity and influence would be enhanced by his trade concession, and his political future seemed assured. He could expect to be rewarded with the governorship of Kentucky, whether it became a state in the Union or a province of Spain. He left New Orleans by ship on September 16, and after a leisurely journey that carried him to Charleston, Richmond, and Philadelphia, he reached home and an anxious wife on February 24, 1788. Ann, a Philadelphia Biddle, had been expecting him for months. She had been "tortured" by his long absence and the ordeal of living among people "that has been brought up so differently from myself." Wilkinson's arrival in Lexington created a sensation, for he appeared with an elaborate four-wheeled carriage drawn by matched horses. Two of the slaves he had purchased were outriders on the team.[4] The pioneer community had seen nothing to match this display of affluence.

Once home, Wilkinson hastened to confide his plans to a select group that included some of the most prominent figures in the District. A consummate intriguer, he revealed varying portions of his schemes, depending upon his estimate of each man's willingness to participate in a Spanish arrangement of some sort. As a consequence, his contemporaries and later historians have never agreed on the goal Wilkinson sought in his scheming. Did he seek separation of Kentucky from both Virginia and the United States, followed by absorption into the Spanish empire? Or was he simply luring the gullible Spanish officials into making important and lucrative trade concessions without ever intending to enter into any sort of political association with Spain? Or did his intentions fall somewhere between those possibilities? Wilkinson left a confused trail, and his true intent may never be known. In his self-serving memoir he scoffed at the more extreme charges. "The idea of alienating Kentucky from the United States, while a prospect of national protection remained, would have been as absurd, as the idea of reducing them to the vassalage of Spain. . . . Indeed, the monstrous extravagance of the thought, is too ludicrous for grave consideration, and could never have originated, with any person who understood the character, genius, and government of the people of the United States."[5]

In his major intrigues during his long and complex career, Wilkinson displayed a genius for avoiding any absolute commitment that would condemn him if the scheme failed. Early in his career he learned the value of keeping open all possible options; James Wilkinson was never a zealot content to becoming a martyr for a lost cause. He was a survivor, and in his dubious association with the "Spanish Conspiracy" he was careful to remain free to move in whatever direction circumstances determined best for him. If in the process he broke promises and avoided commitments and ignored oaths, his honor was flexible enough to bear the strain.

Once back in Kentucky Wilkinson apparently first confided his Spanish scheme to Harry Innes, a key member of the

Harry Innes (1725-1816), one of Wilkinson's "confidential
supporters," was a federal district judge from 1789 until his death.
Courtesy of the J.B. Speed Art Museum, Louisville.

court faction, who was strongly dissatisfied with the Virginia connection and bitterly angered by the Jay-Gardoqui negotiations. Isaac Dunn, Wilkinson's trading partner, and Alexander Scott Bullitt, a Jefferson County planter, were admitted to the cabal. Wilkinson then informed Miro that he had support from the two major parties in Kentucky; if anything happened to him, Innes and Bullitt should be consulted. As he approached other key figures Wilkinson was more cautious in revealing his plans and hopes. He apparently decided that most of them at that time would not go beyond separation from the United States and some vague alliance with Spain. The essential feature of any such alliance would be the free use of the Mississippi River. According to Dunn, leading Kentuckians had declared *"that the direction of the current of the rivers which run in front of their dwellings points clearly to the power to which they ought to ally themselves"* (Dunn's emphasis).[6]

Wilkinson was even more circumspect in his public statements. When talking about the need for a commercial agreement with Spain he was careful not to advocate a political union, either as an ally or as a colony. He stressed Kentucky's vital need for free access to the Mississippi, and he hinted that an independent Kentucky would be able to obtain a favorable agreement. Farmers were ecstatic over his trading success in New Orleans. Tobacco that had sold in the District for two Spanish dollars per hundred weight soared to nine and a half dollars, and the price of other commodities also increased. Of course, others would have to ship through Wilkinson's firm, since he held the only trade permit, but he seemed willing to accept any quantity of goods delivered to him. In January 1789 he dispatched a fleet of twenty-five armed flatboats from Louisville. So much tobacco was shipped that it swamped the market, and Miro begged Wilkinson to curb his exports.[7]

During the year or two following his return from his first New Orleans trip, James Wilkinson was the most popular person in Kentucky. Had the District gained statehood during that period, he could have won easy election to the governorship. Yet there was an undercurrent of suspicion of his motives and his plans in both Kentucky and New Orleans.

Some Kentuckians wondered just how he had been able to obtain the trade concession; what terms had he made? Two young men hired to carry papers on a roundtrip to New Orleans told about a weighted trunk that they were ordered to throw overboard if anyone tried to seize the dispatches in it. Rumors began to circulate that Wilkinson was in the pay of Spain.[8] Governor Miro was not entirely sure of the Kentuckian's reliability, although he had supplied some valuable information. In a June 15, 1788, report to his home government Miro stopped short of complete acceptance. "Although his candor, and the information which I have sought from many who have known him well, seems to assure us that he is working in good earnest," the governor wrote, "yet I am aware that it may be possible that his intention is to enrich himself at our expense, by inflating us with hopes and promises which he knows to be vain. Nevertheless, I have determined to humor him on this occasion."[9]

Before Wilkinson's triumphant return from his trip, Kentucky acquired the District's first newspaper. Thereafter its readers received a somewhat fuller account of the separation movement. The first convention had called for the establishment of a newspaper, and the need had increased since then. After repeated failures to obtain a printer in Philadelphia and Richmond, John Bradford agreed to start a paper if he was guaranteed the contract for public printing. It could have been a rash promise, for he admitted that he "had not the least knowledge of the printing business." Bradford may have visited Kentucky as early as 1779, although details of his early career are uncertain, but he appears to have brought his family from the East in 1785. They settled at Cave Run Creek, about five miles northeast of Lexington, a location that helped him decide to establish his press in Lexington rather than Danville. His brother Fielding had some printing experience, and it was he who brought a press and type from Pittsburgh in 1787. Unfortunately, much of the type got pied during the rough trip from Limestone, and in the first issue, dated August 11, 1787, John Bradford apologized for not producing a better paper. Because of the illness of a more experienced partner, he had been forced to do most of the work, and the mixed type had been a problem. The initial issue of the *Kentucke Gazette* went to some 150 subscribers. The paper was a weekly until 1797, when it began to appear twice weekly. Subscriptions gradually increased, Bradford's five sons helped with the production, and the income from the public printing increased after the advent of statehood.[10]

The first issue of the newspaper appeared about five weeks before the first session of the Fifth Convention, and from the start a considerable portion of its limited space was devoted to political controversy. The editor seldom reported political news. Instead, he printed with little or no editing the lengthy letters sent to him. Usually signed with some assumed name, the authorship must have been apparent to the politically minded readers who pored over the columns of small type. Partisan Ebenezer Brooks ("A Virginian") opposed separation, at least for the present, because he believed the original grievances had been eliminated by the Virginia government. Several members of the court faction responded quickly, the most telling counter coming from Caleb Wallace ("A Kentuckian"). Wallace argued that Kentucky must separate in order to get an adequate defense against the Indians and the free use of the Mississippi River. The state government had not solved either of those vital problems; Kentucky could do better on her own. He charged Brooks with having reversed his position on separation after his "total defeat" on that issue in the first convention.[11] Several others joined in the exchanges.

Delegates to the Fifth Convention were elected in August 1787 at the court days in the various counties. A quorum was present in Danville on September 17, and the convention organized quickly. As usual, Samuel McDowell was elected president and Thomas Todd was appointed secretary. While several partisans were members of the convention, Brooks, John Campbell and Sam Taylor had not been elected. Deprived of their usual leadership, the partisans who opposed separation abstained when the key vote was taken. Humphrey Marshall and Robert Breckinridge were among the leaders of the country faction, but both groups were outnumbered by the twenty-some court men. Wilkinson was absent and McDowell was in the chair, but Harry Innes, John Fowler, Caleb Wallace, Benjamin Sebastian, and Benjamin Logan provided leadership. Little was needed, for there was scant opposition to the decision made. On Saturday, September 22, the convention agreed to accept the terms offered by Virginia in the Second Enabling Act; to have done otherwise might have resulted in an indefinite delay in achieving statehood. The record vote was unanimous, but at least two of the partisans abstained from voting. Representatives were present from the Cumberland settlements to request that they be included in the new state, but their request was not entertained. To have done so would have complicated the separation movement, for North Carolina would have been involved, and another delay would have been inevitable.

The convention also requested Congress to approve the separation and to admit Kentucky into the Union as quickly as possible. In accord with the Enabling Act, the convention set April 1788 for the election of delegates to a July constitutional convention. All free male inhabitants were declared eligible to vote. Partition from Virginia would occur on December 31, 1788. The editor of the *Kentucky Gazette* was asked to publish the election resolutions for six weeks prior to the voting days. "I have hopes our affairs may go on Smoothly in the future," McDowell wrote after the key vote had been taken.[12]

In an effort to secure better representation in Congress, where they believed their interests had often been ignored, the delegates requested Virginia to include someone from the District of Kentucky in the state's congressional delegation, which could number from two to seven. The Virginia General Assembly honored the request by appointing John Brown, senator from the District. Educated at Princeton and the College of William and Mary, Brown had then studied law with Edmund Randolph, George Wythe, and Thomas Jefferson. He and three companions had barely escaped Indians when they rode the Wilderness Trail to Kentucky in 1783. The best trained person in Kentucky at that time, Brown was elected to the Virginia

Senate in 1784, although some of his associates did not think highly of his political skills. Wilkinson told Miro in 1789 that Brown "is a young man of respectable talents, but timid, without political experience, and with very little knowledge of the world." He had been sent to Congress, Wilkinson added, to spy on that body. Youthful in appearance but already portly when he became a Kentuckian, Brown often delayed taking action and agonized over his decisions because he could not judge what was the right thing to do.[13] He was susceptible to influence, and James Wilkinson supplied it.

When Brown arrived in New York City on December 6, 1787, Congress lacked a quorum and was not in session. He soon discovered that the ratification of the new federal constitution and the impending organization of a national government were jeopardizing Kentucky's separation request. Little was being done in Congress while the members and their states waited to see some indication of the nation's political future.

Politically minded Kentuckians had studied carefully the document that had come out of the Philadelphia convention, and many of them were opposed to what they read. Brown wrote a friend that "Kentucky would have much more to fear than to hope from the event." He later changed his opinion; the danger of anarchy was so great that the constitution should be ratified regardless of its weaknesses. Most of his Kentucky friends disagreed.[14]

Wilkinson and the other leaders of the court faction generally opposed the new constitution. Their chief fear was that the federal government would have powers that they hoped to use on the state level. They wanted land cases involving nonresidents to be tried in Kentucky courts; they planned to tax imports to help promote manufacturing; they wanted to take what action was necessary to protect land interests. The constitution under consideration would restrict state powers in too many ways. Furthermore, the eastern states had such a numerical superiority that they would be able to discriminate against the West. In an effort to create opposition to ratification, Harry Innes and seven other members of the court faction sent an open letter to the Fayette County Court on February 29, 1788. (It was also sent to the Mercer County Court and presumably to the other courts as well.) After a general denunciation of the constitution, the letter warned that a government organized under it would abandon the nation's right to free use of the Mississippi River and that Kentucky would be hurt more severely than any other part of the country. The signers of the letter called for a special convention that would instruct the fourteen Kentuckians who would be members of Virginia's ratifying convention later in the year.[15] Obviously they hoped the instructions would be negative.

Partisan spokesmen remained silent, but most members of the country faction supported ratification. They denied that the new government would abandon the Mississippi, and they stressed the need for something better than the Articles of Confederation. Humphrey Marshall took the lead by campaigning actively for a seat in the Virginia convention. Wilkinson and Innes set out to defeat him by circulating scurrilous rumors about him. In a spirited reply published in the February 23, 1788, issue of the *Kentucky Gazette*, Marshall included one Jordan Harris in his counteraccusations. A few days later Harris followed Marshall as he left town and tried to hand him one of a pair of pistols. Marshall refused it, but when Harris started to fire, Marshall, who was on horseback, deflected the weapon with his walking stick. Marshall dismounted and approached Harris, who missed with a second shot. Marshall struck his adversary on the arm with his stick, and Harris turned and ran for town—to get more ammunition, he claimed; because of fright, Marshall declared.

Marshall rejected a formal challenge to a duel—a gentleman did not lower himself to duel with an inferior—but he engaged Harris in a heated exchange in Bradford's paper. Marshall's now famous walking stick, adorned with a blue ribbon, may have helped him win election to the ratifying convention. When Harris proved unable to match Marshall in the newspaper exchanges, Wilkinson published over Harris's name a series of satirical articles to which Marshall replied in kind.[16] The exchange fell well below even the accepted standards of the day, but it provided unusual entertainment for the community.

Well before the Richmond convention gathered on June 2, 1788, vote counters knew that the result would be close. Patrick Henry and George Mason were among the adamant opponents of the federal constitution, and they had many supporters. They feared that the national government would be so strong it would weaken the states. The lack of a bill of rights concerned many members, but it gave proponents of the constitution a good bargaining point: adopt the constitution and we will use its amending process to add what you want. Specific objections were raised to almost every provision in the document. The opponents of ratification may have lost their best chance of rejecting it when the convention voted to debate the provisions clause by clause. Its advocates had feared that one of Patrick Henry's famed orations might sweep the delegates into a negative vote. That danger was decreased in lengthy, detailed debates. The opponents also suffered a serious setback when Edmund Randolph, who had refused to sign the finished document at Philadelphia, finally decided to support it. James Madison, John Marshall, and George Nicholas, soon to move to Kentucky, were among the most determined and effective defenders of ratification.[17]

The vote was expected to be so close that the fourteen Kentuckians might well decide the issue. Although John Brown was not a member, he was lobbied by both sides because it was thought he might be able to influence Kentucky's delegates. Harry Innes warned him that adoption "would be the destruction of our young and flourishing country," but Madison asked Brown to write to the Kentuckians and urge their support for ratification.

In April, Madison wrote Thomas Jefferson, then the American minister to France, that "The real sense of the people of this State cannot be easily ascertained." He had not heard the results from Kentucky, but that District was expected to be divided. Madison was still unsure of the outcome on June 4 when he told an anxious George Washington, "I dare not however speak with certainly as to the decision. Kentucke has been extremely tainted, is supposed to be generally adverse, and every piece of address is going on privately to work on the local interests & prejudices of that & other quarters." A few days later Madison was even more concerned about the Kentucky vote: "There is reason to believe that the event may depend on the Kentucky members, who seem to lean more against than in favor of the Constitution. The business is in the most ticklish state that can be imagined."

Later in the convention young James Breckinridge, who had journeyed to Richmond to hear the debates (which exceeded his expectations), reported the Kentuckians' concerns to his brother John, who was already thinking of moving west. "The Ky. members, on whom the decision seems greatly to depend, seem determined to pursue the opinions they had before leaving, that it would accomplish their internal ruin and destruction. They worry about the necessity of going to a court in a distant part of the land to decide their land claims. Also concerned over the navigation of the Miss. which they feel would be to the interest of the Northern States to prohibit." Once committed to ratification, John Brown extended his lobbying to include at least one member who was not from Kentucky. "I am at a loss to account for the general dissatisfication of that District," he wrote Matthew Walsont, "to a System of Government upon which in my opinion the peace & Glory of the United States depends." He had examined the constitution carefully, Brown said, and had found nothing that was injurious to Kentucky's interests. Congress and the eastern states were no longer hostile on the Mississippi question; Kentucky had nothing to fear in that regard. The national political system was in such a wretched condition, Brown continued, that "a change must take place & in my opinion we cannot under our present circumstances obtain better than the plan proposes." In the convention debates George Nicholas also tried to assuage the westerners' fears. He owned land in Kentucky, and he expected to move there in the near future; would he favor a form of government that would harm his future home?[18]

The Kentuckians did not participate actively in the debates as the convention argued its way to a fateful decision. Virginia had the largest population of any state, and it was difficult to imagine a successful government that did not include the Old Dominion. If Virginia rejected the constitution, some states that had ratified might well withdraw. The issue was settled on June 25 when the convention voted 89-79 to ratify the federal constitution, although it called for several amendments to remedy some perceived defects, the most important being the addition of a bill of rights. Noltey Conn of Bourbon County was either not present or abstained from voting; no explanation was given. Of the other thirteen Kentucky delegates, only Humphrey Marshall, Robert Breckinridge, and Rice Bullock voted for ratification. The other ten remained adamant in their opposition.[19] The shift from one national government to another caused another complication in the often delayed separation movement.

Some Kentuckians who might have been delegates to the Richmond convention refused the opportunity because they had been selected for the Sixth Convention that was scheduled to meet in Danville on July 28, 1788. No one could predict how long the ratifying convention would take, and the trip back to Kentucky was still long, although perhaps somewhat less dangerous than it had once been. The essential steps had been taken toward statehood, and delegates probably anticipated a reasonably harmonious meeting. Brown had introduced the petition for statehood in Congress in February, and it had been assigned to committee for the preparation of a bill. He was sure that it would be approved, but as the weeks passed without action, Brown began to fear that it would be delayed, perhaps until the fate of the new constitution was known. He heard several objections to a quick admission. Some Congressmen did not believe that the Articles of Confederation government had the power to admit new states; that power was specifically granted in Article IV of the constitution being ratified. Sectional divisions had appeared on several issues, and some of the northeastern states were reluctant to admit a state that was sure to vote with their opponents. Some members feared

that the admission of Kentucky would jeopardize the ratification of the constitution in certain northeastern states.

The Second Enabling Act had set a July 4, 1788, deadline
for congressional action. At last, on July 3 the committee
presented resolutions approving the Virginia-Kentucky compact and admitting Kentucky to the Union on January 1, 1789.
But then the body voted to postpone the admission because the
new constitution had been ratified by the necessary number of
states, and it would be "manifestly improper" for Congress to
usurp the power of its successor. As an expression of opinion,
Congress added that Kentucky should be admitted as soon as
possible. That sop was cold comfort to Brown and to most
Kentuckians when they learned that there would be yet another in their series of delays.

Angered by this action, Brown explored a possible alter-
native. He may have held talks with Don Diego de Gardoqui,
Spain's first envoy to the United States, as early as April; their
conversations became potentially more meaningful during the
summer. Brown reported the gist of the exchanges to such
trusted associates as Samuel McDowell and George Muter.
Brown said that Gardoqui had told him that Kentucky could
not obtain the desired trade concessions on the Mississippi
River as long as it was a part of the United States. But if an
independent Kentucky negotiated with him, he had authority
to reach a mutually agreeable solution. Brown's letter to
Muter was published two years later in the *Kentucky Gazette* of
September 4, 1790. It appeared to indicate that Brown was
actively seeking independent status for Kentucky in 1788;
Brown's political opponents plagued him with that charge for
the rest of his political life.[20]

These developments terminated the short-lived Sixth Convention. A quorum was not formed on Monday, July 28, 1788,
but on Tuesday Samuel McDowell and Thomas Todd were
returned to their usual positions, the rules of the last convention were adopted, and standing committees were appointed.
Before adjournment until nine o'clock on Wednesday morning,
Todd reported that "Sundry Papers and Resolutions of the
Congress of the United States, addressed to Samuel McDowell,

Esquire, late President of the Convention in Kentucky, was read and ordered to lie on the Clerk's Table." John Brown's news of what had transpired in Congress had arrived. McDowell withheld from the convention Brown's report on his talks with Gardoqui; privately he informed other members of the court faction of the Spaniard's offer to an independent Kentucky.[21]

The import of the news seemed clear. Since the time limit set by the Second Enabling Act for congressional action had expired, the convention's authority was terminated. Nothing could be done until Virginia passed another act. But some of the incensed members were not willing to submit themselves and the District of Kentucky again to the procedure that after years of effort had failed to produce statehood. Humphrey Marshall later recalled that there was "the most deep-felt vexation, a share of ill temper bordering on disaffection to the legal course of things; and some strong symptoms of assuming *independent government.*" Caleb Wallace got the floor as soon as the Wednesday session opened. Since the powers of the convention had been annulled, he moved "that it was the duty of this Convention as the Representatives of the people to proceed to frame a Constitution of Government for this District and to submit the same to their consideration with such advice relative thereto as emergency suggests."[22]

The committee-of-the-whole considered his resolution and related matters on through Wednesday and again on Thursday. Wallace, Wilkinson, Innes and Sebastian, among the most outspoken advocates of separation, condemned the easterners who were held responsible for the congressional rejection. Innes was so angry that he felt "like shedding blood." John Edwards, a leader of the country faction, was the chief spokesman for restraint and moderation. He suggested that perhaps the impending change in the national government did justify the delay. If the members were unwilling to repeat the application process, they should refer the matter to the people before embarking upon a drastic course of action that the people had not approved. They had been elected to be a constitutional convention, he reminded his colleagues; they should not attempt anything else before hearing from their constituents. An unknown partisan suggested that the militia captains could poll their men to ascertain public opinion, but Thomas Marshall led the successful opposition to that proposal. He argued that, despite the unwelcome delay, the convention method was the best way to measure the will of the people.[23]

After a brisk discussion, committee chairman Isaac Shelby presented a report on Thursday that was adopted without open dissent. It admitted that the action of Congress had left the convention without authority to act. But "being anxious for the safety and prosperity of ourselves and constituents," they recommended that each county elect five members to a convention that would meet in Danville on the first Monday in November 1788. To avoid delay if another convention was needed, this one would exercise power until January 1, 1790. The people were asked to delegate to their representatives "full powers to take such measures for obtaining admission of the District as a separate and independent member of the United States of America, and the navigation of the river Mississippi as may appear most conducive to these important purposes." The delegates to the November convention would also be authorized "to form a Constitution of Government for the District, and organize the same when they shall Judge it necessary, or to do and accomplish whatever, on a consideration of the State of the District, may in their Opinion promote its interests." No previous convention had been granted such broad powers; the next convention was to expedite the creation of a state and the formation of a government for it.

The resolutions also contained regulations for the election and the meeting of the convention. A quorum would be a simple majority of the members. In the absence of a quorum, as few as five members could adjourn for up to five days, then, if necessary, for a period not to exceed a month. The most surprising provision extended the right to vote to all free male inhabitants, although the Virginia act of 1769, which remained in effect for several decades, had a freehold property qualification. Fifty acres were required for unsettled land, twenty-five acres if the owner had a house at least twelve feet square. A house of the same minimum size on a town lot also met the requirement. This Kentucky expansion of suffrage was one of the most radical moves of the pre-statehood era. Designed to gain support for the separation movement, it set a standard that many states did not match until well into the next century. The convention completed its preparations on July 31 and ended its short session after voting thanks to its clerk and to John Brown for "his faithful attention to their Interests in Congress." [24]

The brief period between the Sixth and Seventh conventions was filled with an unusual amount of animated political discussion. The mass of the people were not actively involved, but the leaders of the political factions filled the columns of the *Kentucky Gazette* with heated epistles. Ebenezer Brooks ("Cornplanter") presented the partisans' case against separation in the issue of September 13, 1788. It should not be attempted without the consent of Congress, and he warned that statehood would result in higher taxes and a reduced chance of securing free use of the Mississippi River. Harry Innes ("A Farmer") insisted in the October 18 issue that the repeated votes for severing ties with Virginia demonstrated strong public support for that goal. In an effort to forestall a possible hostile tactic, he warned against seeking instructions from the people; the delegates whom they selected to represent them in the next convention were best qualified "to decide on *knotty* and intricate points of State policy." Humphrey Marshall later claimed that the resolutions adopted at the Sixth Convention had aroused suspicions about the "Spanish Conspiracy." He did not explain why country faction members did not oppose the resolutions or bring up that issue during the campaign. [25]

The most surprising public communication during this interlude between conventions was a handbill signed by Chief Justice George Muter, which reached a wider audience when published in Bradford's newspaper on October 18. Muter, a native of Scotland, was then nearing sixty years of age. Despite the position he held, many who knew him were not impressed by either his abilities or his talent for leadership. A subjective historian wrote that "his patriotism was indisputable. But he was vacillating as compared with the strong men with whom he came in contact, easily influenced as events proved, and neither wise enough to keep counsel nor vigorous enough to permanently command the respect of contending parties." As a member of the court faction he had been a loyal follower of his more assertive associates. But he had moved from the Danville area and had become a neighbor of Thomas Marshall and his clan near Frankfort. In his new habitat Muter soon fell under the influence of the Marshalls. When he received John Brown's letter that seemed to indicate a desire for an immediate, unilateral separation, a disturbed Muter showed it to Colonel Marshall, who supported legal separation with the full approval of Virginia. The Colonel persuaded Muter to issue a handbill over his name, although Marshall was probably the primary author. The Muter manifesto warned the public that, under Virginia law, drafting a constitution and establishing a government without permission constituted high treason. Furthermore, the new federal constitution prohibited the formation of a new state without the consent of Congress and the parent state. The people should instruct their delegates to the next convention on the course that should be followed to prevent an active minority from taking drastic and illegal action. In terms of leadership, the court faction suffered little from Muter's defection, but his shift had considerable symbolic value. It encouraged the opponents of the court men, it contributed directly to the formulation of sets of instructions for some of the county delegations, and it clarified the legality issue on which much of the election campaign revolved.[26]

Back in May, Wilkinson had told Miro that before the July convention he would ascertain the opinions of the delegates and the influence each possessed. "When this is done," he continued, "after having previously come to an understanding with two or three individuals capable of assisting me, I shall disclose so much of our great scheme as may appear opportune, according to circumstances, and I have no doubt but that it will meet with a favorable reception." When a new government was formed, "I doubt not but they will name a political agent to treat of the affair in which we are engaged, and I think that all this will be done by the month of March next." Meanwhile, Wilkinson concluded, he would attempt to execute any orders that Miro might send.[27] Events had checked the execution of that plan but had not necessarily killed it, for the extensive powers delegated to the Seventh Convention would enable the members to take whatever action they deemed necessary. But who would control the convention?

Some of the campaigning for seats in the convention was spirited, although most of the members of the previous convention who sought re-election won. Wilkinson was one of the candidates who encountered problems. On the fifth and last day of the Fayette County election he was doing so poorly that he had to disavow violent separation; he pledged to follow the will of the people. He eked out a victory, but Caleb Wallace was left at home. Innes, McDowell, and Sebastian were returned but John Fowler was not. Partisan Ebenezer Brooks was also denied a seat. John Brown had returned home from Congress in time to become a member. He had become skeptical of the Spanish scheme, but Wilkinson apparently persuaded him to remain with the court faction.[28]

A quorum was not present on Monday, November 3, 1788, but on Tuesday the convention organized; as usual, Samuel McDowell was selected president and Thomas Todd was appointed clerk. The usual housekeeping committees were formed, the rules of the previous convention were adopted, and the congressional papers received by McDowell were ordered to lie on the clerk's table, where they could be examined. When the convention went into committee-of-the-whole on Wednesday, Wilkinson was elected chairman, a position he continued to hold as the members shifted frequently between convention and committee. The official record does not report debates, but an argument apparently erupted in the committee over the powers possessed by the convention and their source. Muter, Marshall, Edwards, and others insisted that the convention could do nothing except petition Virginia for permission to become independent and to form a state government. Wilkinson, Brown, Sebastian, and Innes denied that such permission was necessary; the convention possessed sovereign power, derived from the people, and it could declare independence, draft a constitution, and provide for the opening of the Mississippi River without obtaining permission from any body. During the discussion someone discovered that the resolutions of the July convention were not legal since they had not been referred to committee before being adopted. Another argument then broke out over the need to send resolutions to committee; could not the convention act directly when it wanted to do so? The Wilkinson faction won that point, and the committee-of-the-whole rose, turned itself back into the convention, then referred the resolutions to the committee, which approved them and returned them to the convention for final, legal passage. Before adjourning for the day the convention decided to send "a decent and respectful Address" to the Virginia General Assembly asking for another act that would perhaps finally result in separation. A committee was appointed to draft the address, and petitions from Mercer and Madison counties for the opening of the Mississippi River were sent to the committee-of-the-whole.[29]

The decisive point of the convention came when Wilkinson made his major effort to separate Kentucky without prior permission from Virginia and Congress. Since Spain would not deal with the United States on the Mississippi question, he told his colleagues, Kentucky must act alone. Wilkinson proposed that Kentucky draft a constitution, declare independence from Virginia, and organize a government. If terms were satisfactory, Kentucky might join the Union. The implication was clear; if terms were unsatisfactory, Kentucky might turn to Spain. Then Wilkinson remarked that a gentleman who was present had important information regarding the Mississippi question. He looked at John Brown, then relinquished the floor.

Wilkinson obviously expected Brown to give a strong endorsement of his proposal, backed by a report on his conversations with Gardoqui. That information might be enough to sweep the convention into an immediate declaration of independence. But Brown had found that the northeastern opposition was not as great as he had feared, and that the sentiment in Kentucky for unilateral separation was less than he had expected. When he reluctantly responded to a member's request that he divulge the information to which Wilkinson had alluded, Brown said that he did not feel free to discuss in detail his conversations with the Spanish minister. But, he was reported to have added, "this much in general, he would venture to inform the convention, that, *provided we are unanimous, every thing we could wish for, is within our reach.*" [30]

"Brown's hesitating words broke the momentum toward independence," concluded Brown's biographer. Wilkinson must have been dismayed by Brown's defection, but he took the floor again. He had some knowledge of the Mississippi question, Wilkinson declared, and he proceeded to read a fifteen- to twenty-page manuscript. It was probably a carefully edited version of the memorial he had given the Spanish authorities in New Orleans, with all references to his Spanish associations omitted. As he finished a page, Wilkinson handed it to Sebastian, who was seated near him. The manuscript was not delivered to the clerk, and it soon disappeared. [31] This may well have been the turning point in the separation movement, the moment when James Wilkinson saw one of his options begin to vanish.

When the session opened on Thursday, November 6, the convention received a favorable report from the committee-of-the-whole on the two county petitions. Another committee was appointed to draft the address to Congress. Edwards then reported an address to the General Assembly written by a special committee; Wilkinson was probably its major author. After it and a proposed amendment were ordered to lie on the clerk's table, John Brown offered a resolution: "That it is the wish, and intent of the good people of this District to separate from the State of Virginia and that the same be erected into an Independent member of the Federal Union." While the resolution did not say that Kentucky must accept the terms agreed upon with Virginia, it did commit the District to membership in the United States. The resolution did not pass, however. [32]

The brief Friday meeting did not produce action on any of the pending measures, but on Saturday the convention adopted a Wilkinson resolution. Its preamble declared that opinions were so badly divided that it was doubtful if any plan could be drafted that could obtain a majority in a situation "perplexed with doubts and surrounded by difficultys." Therefore, in order "to avoid error, and to obtain truth, to remove the Jealousys which have infected society, and to restore that spirit of harmony and concord, on which the prosperity of all depends," a committee should draft an address to the people of the District. They should be asked to instruct the delegates at the next session of the convention how to proceed with the important tasks before them. The resolution was accepted and a seven-man committee, including Wilkinson, was appointed to write the address. Then, before adjourning until Monday, the address to the General Assembly was read, amended, and referred to the committee-of-the-whole.[33]

Over the short weekend, petitions with three hundred to five hundred signatures opposing violent separation were secured, chiefly in the Lexington area. Joseph Crockett presented them to the convention on Monday morning. The petitions effectively blocked any further moves by Wilkinson. He had called for instructions from the people, but he had never expected such an immediate negative response. He presented an address, "To the United States in Congress Assembled," that was much more temperate than some of his earlier works. This "humble petition" called upon the "Fathers!—Fellow Citizens!—and Guardians of our rights!" to secure for Kentuckians their natural right to free use of the Mississippi. "If you will be really our fathers," he implored, "stretch forth your hands to save us. . . . Do not cut us off from your body." Wilkinson also presented an address directed to the General Assembly. Shorter and less emotional than the appeal to Congress, it asked for the passage of another enabling act so Kentucky could "obtain an independent Government and be admitted into the confederation, as a member of the Federal Union, upon such terms and conditions as to you may appear just and equitable." It asked quick action to secure "the final completion of the business," and it requested the legislature to urge Congress to take speedy action upon both statehood and the free use of the Mississippi.[34] The mild tone of the document was in sharp contrast to some of the earlier demands. It must have been a bitter pill for its author.

Between the introduction of these two addresses, the busy Wilkinson also presented for the committee-of-the-whole an "Address to the People of the District." The convention gave it a formal reading, then returned it to the committee, where it apparently died. It was not included in the journal, and the convention ended its session after voting thanks to General James Wilkinson for the address which he had presented to the Spanish authorities and "for the regard which he therein manifested for the Interest of the Western Country." Humphrey Marshall wrote that his "adherents were pleased to stick this new plume in his cap"; his opponents saw it "as an harmless ensign." That tribute paid, the convention adjourned until the first Monday in August 1789. To provide for possible contingencies, the president, with the advice of three members or upon the request of five members, could advance the meeting date. If the president died or was otherwise unavailable, any five members could convene the convention.[35]

Wilkinson's defeat was not readily apparent to those who did not know of his Spanish plans. He had been the most active member of the convention and its major penman, and he appeared to be at the height of his popularity. In reality, his influence was declining. He had not been able to push the convention into precipitate action, and the addresses he crafted did not reflect his hopes. He had to explain to his Spanish associates that "the great question" had to be postponed until the people, angered by more delays in attaining statehood, were prepared to accept it. Wilkinson insisted that Muter and Marshall were the only leading Kentuckians who were hostile to his plans, and he said that their support could be won by $2,500 properly applied. But his support was eroding even within the court faction. Muter had departed, and Brown seemed likely to follow. McDowell and Fowler appeared to have lost interest in the cause, and Wallace had not been elected to the last convention. No answer had been made to the memorial that Miro had sent to Spain in 1787, so Wilkinson lacked specific inducements with which to hold his faltering troops in place. Innes and Sebastian were his most dependable supporters, but how much longer could he be sure of their loyalty?[36]

The colonization scheme to which Wilkinson turned after the Seventh Convention adjourned was at least in part an effort to obtain land that could be awarded to those men who would follow his leadership. Of course he hoped to secure a great estate for himself. He, Innes, Brown, Sebastian, and Isaac Dunn petitioned Gardoqui for a 60,000-acre grant on the Yazoo and Mississippi rivers. It would help repay them for their efforts on behalf of Spain, Wilkinson wrote. And it could be "a place of refuge for me and my adherents" if they were forced to flee from the United States. He opposed Spanish efforts to attract American settlers to the New Madrid area, for it might conflict with his scheme. Miro agreed to halt that settlement, although later it was allowed to continue.[37]

John Brown wrote his friend Madison on November 23, 1788, that the convention had decided to renew the request for statehood. "This Country was too much disturbed by faction & divided in political opinions to admit of the adoption of any other measure had it even been thought necessary," Brown added. The request had gone to the Virginia legislature, and Kentuckians expected another enabling act to be passed soon.[38]

FOUR

The Later Conventions

Virginia's Second Enabling Act became void when Congress in July 1788 refused to admit Kentucky to the Union. On December 29, 1788, the General Assembly passed the Third Enabling Act because "the good people of Kentucky" desired it and because the "remote situation" of the District made separation expedient. During the court days of May 1789, each of Kentucky's counties would elect five delegates to a convention (the eighth) that was to meet in Danville on July 20, 1789. Much of the new act was similar to the previous one, but the terms included some important changes that aroused strong opposition in the West. Kentucky was to "take upon itself a just proportion of the public and domestic debt of this commonwealth," and unlocated lands appropriated for military and other services to the state were to remain under Virginia's jurisdiction until Congress admitted Kentucky to the Union. If the Eighth Convention agreed to the new terms, it would fix a date after November 1, 1790, when separation would occur, provided that before September 1, 1790, Congress agreed to add Kentucky to the Union. To prevent a period of anarchy, the convention could provide for a constitutional convention and could determine what Virginia laws would remain in effect until the new state government could act. The joint committee for the settlement of disputes, provided for in the Second Enabling Act, was omitted.[1]

The harsher provisions of this act encouraged opponents of

separation, who saw an opportunity to block it. Much of the animated discussion on the issue was contained in the pages of the *Kentucky Gazette*. Samuel Taylor ("A Real Friend to the People") presented the most comprehensive of the partisan assaults on separation. He denied that the mass of the people had ever supported separation; the gentlemen who desired detachment from Virginia had never dared seek election on that specific issue. Taylor charged that there had been "an actual attempt made to usurp a government independent of the general Union," in addition to "frequent overtures" in that direction. Members of the court faction made a quiet alliance with Taylor and the other partisans, and they used the stringent provisions of the new Enabling Act as a key point in their appeals to the voters.[2]

Two astute political observers described the political situation in the spring of 1789. Although James Madison had never visited Kentucky, he was deeply interested in the western counties and their future. He wrote Thomas Jefferson in late March that "some of the leaders in Kentucky are known to favor the idea of connection with Spain. The people are as yet inimical to it. Their future disposition will depend upon the measures of the new Government."[3]

Especially interesting was a detailed report from George Nicholas, who had recently moved to Kentucky and established a lucrative law practice. Although only thirty-six years old in 1789, his career had included study at the College of William and Mary, active service in the American Revolution, during which he rose to the rank of colonel, and membership in the Virginia House of Delegates and the ratifying convention of 1788. Nicholas had assisted James Madison and George Mason in opposing state aid to religion, and he had played a major role in securing ratification of the federal constitution. A large bald head and a corpulent body ("a plum pudding with legs on it") made him appear older than he was; men his senior often called him "Old Nicholas." Often taciturn in mixed company or large groups, he was a fascinating conversationalist in small male gatherings. His brick home in Lexington and his farm house near Danville were both noted for their open hospitality. When Nicholas crossed the mountains and settled in Mercer County he swore that his political days were over, that he would remain aloof from politics in his new home. But he could hardly avoid observing what was happening, and in May 1789 he sent Madison his analysis of the political situation in Kentucky.

Nicholas reported that the leading men in the District denied that they favored separation from the United States; their goal, they insisted, was to establish a state government, which both Virginia and the United States had earlier approved, without further delay. Those who were believed to favor independence from the United States "remained silent in the Convention and have continued so since." But "*It is said*," Nicholas continued, "that most of them are now opposed to a seperation from Virginia." He warned, however, that the changes in the last Enabling Act might have resulted in some shift of opinion in the District. The opponents of this group contended that the group wanted to prevent a legal separation until they could secure independence that might lead to important Spanish concessions. Nicholas warned that the situation was critical.

He summed up the situation as he saw it. "I believe a majority of the District wish a seperation from Virginia but to remain a member of the Union and I am satisfied that a few proper steps taken by the General Government will make it more popular here than in any place in America." The first step, Nicholas said, was to secure the free navigation of the Mississippi River. "If the Delaware was blocked up would they not interfere?" he asked in reference to easterners who showed little concern for the Mississippi issue. Next, he warned, the general government must provide adequate protection from the Indians or see more and more Americans move into Spanish territory, where they could feel safe. He refuted the eastern charge that the Kentuckians, not the Indians, were usually the aggressors. A federal court should also be established in Kentucky at once. Overall, Nicholas continued, the trouble was that "a proper idea as to the importance of this country has not yet been taken up. Be assured that no great length of time will

George Nicholas (1754?-1799), a latecomer to Kentucky, was the primary author of the 1792 constitution. *Courtesy of The Filson Club, Louisville.*

elapse before her inhabitants will be more numerous than those of all the other parts of Virginia." The westerners would live under any government that obtained their rights for them. He was attached to the Union, Nicholas assured his friend, but "if I am disappointed in my expectations from the justice and policy of the new Government . . . I shall be ready to join in any other Mode for obtaining our rights." Further delay in securing their "reasonable demands" would be dangerous, he concluded. Men should "recall how willingly Great Britain would have acceded to the terms first demanded by America after she had in vain attempted to subjugate her. Reasonable terms when once rejected will not give satisfaction."[4]

A number of prominent easterners in addition to Madison were much concerned over the Kentucky situation. President-elect Washington was among those who feared a permanent break. Ironically, he arranged to correspond by code with Harry Innes, one of James Wilkinson's strongest supporters, who was to uncover information about the attempts to sow "seeds of disaffection" in Kentucky. Washington also urged Thomas Marshall to keep him informed about the alarming events in the West. In order to correspond freely, Washington suggested that they might also use a cipher.[5] If the danger of violent separation had abated by that time, it was not clearly evident to all concerned persons.

The Eighth Convention was dominated by the country and partisan factions when it met in Danville on Monday, July 20, 1789. With most of the court leaders missing, the caliber of the membership was lower than in previous meetings. James Brown, the brother of John Brown, commented wryly that "the folly of the District was fully represented. Dullness, the offspring of Ignorance, presided during the whole session save when an inroad was made on her domain by the noisy, pert impertinence of Sam Taylor." A visitor to Danville who also observed the session reported "no able speakers" among the "Convention Gentlemen." Samuel McDowell, apparently the only leader in the court faction who was elected to the convention, was again made president, and Thomas Todd was again employed as clerk. They gave some degree of continuity to a body in which at least twenty members were serving in their first convention. The standard housekeeping committees were appointed, and a new officer was added when Joshua Barbee became sergeant-at-arms.

On Tuesday morning the clerk was ordered to call the roll at each session and to read "with an Audible Voice" the minutes of the previous day. The first substantive business came when the convention began consideration of the Enabling Act of December 1788. That act, the pertinent resolutions of Congress, and the Federal Constitution were read and ordered to be sent to the committee-of-the-whole. With Isaac Shelby presiding, the committee worked on the materials, then was granted additional time to continue its consideration.[6]

On Wednesday morning James Marshall of Woodford County moved that Kentucky separate from Virginia and become an independent member of the Union. Shelby continued to preside over the committee-of-the-whole through Wednesday and into Thursday, July 23, when the convention discharged the committee from further consideration of the measure. Messages from Congress to the governor of Virginia, from the governor to the county lieutenant of Mercer County, and from the county lieutenants were received and tabled for consideration. Then the convention again resolved itself into a committee-of-the-whole to consider the state of the District. When Shelby reported to the convention, a resolution was read, amended, and adopted. It protested that the terms of the Third Enabling Act had been "materially altered" from those previously agreed upon and were "injurious to and inadmissable by the people of this District." By a 25 to 13 vote the convention agreed to request the General Assembly to restore the terms of the Second Act. In an unusual move that reflected the seriousness with which the convention viewed the issue, the votes were recorded in the journal. A committee was appointed to prepare an appropriate address to the General Assembly.[7]

On Friday morning George Muter presented to the legislature the proposed memorial, after which it was read twice and sent to the committee-of-the-whole. When Joseph Crockett of Fayette County reported for the committee later in the day, he introduced several amendments, which were adopted. In its final form, the memorial charged that the restrictions placed on Kentucky in the Third Act would deny it the sovereign power that belonged to any independent state and would make Kentucky inferior to the other states. The convention therefore requested a return to the terms previously agreed upon by the state and the District. The members also voted to have the presiding officer call the convention back into session as soon as another enabling act was passed. The president was authorized to convene the convention for other reasons upon the advice of three members; or, if the president could not act, any ten members could do so. The delegates from each county were directed to take a census of their county's population before the convention met again. They were to meet at their respective courthouses in October to lay out precinct boundaries, then each of the five delegates would be responsible for taking the count in his precinct. As an indication of the growing interest in local manufacturing, the members also passed a resolution deploring Kentuckians' use of high-value imported goods.[8]

Before adjourning, the convention also decided to protest to the federal government about continued Indian depredations. In 1788 each county had agreed to send out six to twelve scouts and to put one-twelfth of its militia on active duty as rangers, but the counties had not been able to finance those defensive measures. Governor Beverly Randolph told the county lieutenants that, since the federal government had agreed to station troops in the West, the state would no longer attempt to defend the frontier: "You will immediately discharge all the scouts and rangers employed in your county." In future they should notify the nearest federal officer of an Indian attack and let him deal with the problem. The thin screen of troops was inadequate to stop Indian incursions, and on June 1, 1790, George Thompson complained bitterly to Madison, who was burdened with the troubles of a number of Kentuckians. "I declare to you that almost every day while in that Country I could hear of some body being massacred or taken by those inhuman Savages, and the number of Horses stolen by them is incredible to relate." He demanded to know what Congress was going to do about the danger. To protest the state's withdrawal of aid, the convention created a committee of seventeen members to prepare a strong remonstrance. A gentleman who commented that "Our Indian affairs seem to engage the attention of the common people & a Separation that of the leading men" understated the convention's concern over more adequate protection.[9] That was a major concern of practically everyone in the District.

The contentious partisans voted against separation, but they also opposed the objections to the Third Enabling Act, although the complaints against the terms of the act, if adopted, would again delay implementation of separation. Defeated in the convention, some of the partisans sought to delay the break with Virginia by questioning the validity of the convention's actions. Samuel Taylor and others presented the General Assembly with an anti-separation petition signed by several hundred Kentuckians. The petition charged that "it was not the will of the good people of said District that the same should be erected into an independent state." Separation might "injure us until time shall be no more," for a new government would "only serve as one of Pharos lean kine to devour our liberty, whilst it can be of no security to our property." Had the late convention been truly representative of the people, the petition declared, it would have rejected separation.[10]

This partisan protest failed to delay the separation movement. By this time many eastern Virginians must have been as weary of the protracted negotiations as were most of the westerners. On December 18, 1789, the General Assembly enacted the Fourth Enabling Act, modifying or deleting sections of the Third Act to which the convention had objected. Kentucky was to assume a just share of the debt of the United States but not of the Virginia public debt. In addition, Kentucky was to be responsible for redeeming the certificates issued to finance Indian expeditions for the defense of the District after January 1, 1785. The period during which Virginia could grant warrants for Kentucky lands was extended by a year, to September

1, 1791, but Virginia's right to dispose of unlocated Kentucky lands was terminated as of May 1, 1792, instead of running to the date of actual statehood. The six-member joint committee to settle disputes that had been eliminated in the Third Act was reinstated.

Assuming—and hoping—that the Fourth Act would be acceptable to the prickly Kentuckians, the General Assembly set another schedule for the parting. Delegates to a Ninth Convention were to be elected at the county court days in May 1790 by the free white males over twenty-one years of age. Each county was to elect five delegates, who must have resided in the District for at least a year. The convention would meet in Danville on July 26, 1790. If, once again, it determined that the people wanted separation, the convention would select a date posterior to November 1, 1791, for consummation—provided that prior to that date Congress had given its consent. The Ninth Convention could then call a constitutional convention that would meet between November 1, 1791, and the date chosen for the final separation.[11] This act proved satisfactory, and it was the one under which the District of Kentucky became the Commonwealth of Kentucky.

When George Nicholas reported to James Madison on the work of the Eighth Convention, he said that a temporary union between the adamant opponents of separation and those who objected to some provisions of the Third Enabling Act had created a majority in the body. Those opposing them had wanted to go forward with separation without more delay; they asserted that the changes in the Third Enabling Act were too minor to justify delay, that objections to the terms were merely excuses for stalling the movement. Nicholas warned that if Spain's liberal immigration policy was not checked it would depopulate Kentucky and the West. Governor Manuel Gayoso's promises of freedom of religion and a democratic form of government would eliminate most of the objections Kentuckians had to being under Spanish rule. In addition, Gayoso promised immigrants a great economic future. Such promises, Nicholas wrote, were in sharp contrast to the neglect of the West by its central government. Among other failures, the national government had not provided the Indians with the goods that would make their plundering unnecessary. Nor had the government provided adequate military protection; a few posts scattered along the Ohio River could not prevent Indians from entering Kentucky at will.

A year later, after Madison tried to assure his friend that the federal government had good intentions and would help solve the problems, Nicholas responded by listing a number of alleged advantages of independence from the United States. "These are the thoughts of the most enlightened men amongst us," Nicholas insisted, "but such thoughts as they only give utterance to in whispers; because it is yet hoped and believed that you will do us justice." If those hopes should be lost, Madison could imagine what the results might be.[12]

James Wilkinson was not a member of the Eighth Convention, but even if he had been he could have done little to retard the movement toward statehood. Much of his influence had been lost by the defeat of the previous year and the persistent rumors of some unsavory plot in which he was involved. His financial plight was becoming desperate, and it tarnished his economic acumen. He had not received the benefits hoped for from Spain, but perhaps a second trip to New Orleans would be more successful than the first had been. To have any chance of procuring profitable concessions from Spanish officials, Wilkinson had to convince them that he was still able to direct the course of events in Kentucky in addition to supplying information about the area and its people. His letters to Miro continued to be optimistic even after the setback in the Seventh Convention. "I have it in my power," he wrote confidently in early 1789, "to carry the great Body of our most opulent and respectable Citizens, wherever I may lead in person."

By the spring Wilkinson had decided to make another personal appeal for assistance. He left Louisville on June 5 and reached the Crescent City about the first of July. As he sought to convince Miro and other key officials of his value to the cause of Spain and his need for financial assistance, he wrote a "Second Memorial" in which he made his case.[13] Written on September 17, 1789, this document tried to convince Miro and others with power to influence policy decisions that modifications to Wilkinson's previous plans were actually beneficial. The gist of his argument was contained in a lengthy sentence. "It will be more useful to the Court of Spain to lay aside the idea of receiving the people of Kentucky under the dominion of His Majesty, and to employ all indirect means to cause the separation of this section of country from the United States, which would likely be followed by a connection with Spain to the exclusion of any other power, Kentucky enjoying the right of self-power; and at the same time to promote emigration to Louisiana." Another approach was necessary, Wilkinson explained, because the creation of a new government in the United States had inspired confidence that it might be stronger than its predecessor.

Wilkinson could not resist asserting that the situation would have been much different had Spain followed his earlier suggestions. Spain needed Kentucky as a barrier against the possible expansion of the United States and Great Britain, Wilkinson continued, and that could be achieved only through the establishment of a separate Kentucky. Spain must use pensions and other rewards to attract the support of the prominent men who could promote that goal. That prospect might appear improbable at the moment, but the Kentuckian provided hope for it in a splendid burst of rhetoric: "Let us not be deceived by appearances; black clouds may soon gather over the heads of those whose sky is now most brilliant, and in the midst of the deceitful calm they enjoy, the tempest that is to overwhelm them has perhaps already begun to brew."

He followed this promise with an impassioned plea for money. "I have employed my time, my property, and all my faculties in promoting the interests of the Spanish monarchy," he complained; "by reason of this conduct I have exposed myself to the wrath of the American Union, without knowing whether my person would be protected, whether I would be indemnified for the loss of my property, or whether His Catholic Majesty would compensate me for my labors." While he abhorred "the idea of venality," the future of his wife and their three small children justified his request. "Modesty, delicacy, and self-esteem all forbid that I should set an estimate upon my own worth," Wilkinson declared, but he was able to repress those traits long enough to request a military commission and at least $7,000.[14]

Miro, in response to this memorial, requested more information on Wilkinson's claim that through payments he could secure the support and services of prominent Kentuckians. On September 18 the Kentucky intriguer made out his famous "List of Characters in Kentucky, worthy to be engaged in the Interests of his Catholic Majesty." With admirable impartiality, Wilkinson included the names of some of his most implacable foes. The list was catholic, a "Who's Who" of Kentucky politicians of that era. Inclusion was unsought and unwanted. Wilkinson grouped its members in four categories. "My confidential supporters" were Harry Innes, Benjamin Sebastian, John Brown, Caleb Wallace, and John Fowler. Each was recommended for an annual pension of $1,000. Next were those who favored separation from the United States and an amiable connection with Spain. Benjamin Logan, Isaac Shelby, and James Garrard deserved $800 annually. A less decided group included William Wood, Henry Lee, Robert Johnston, and Richard Taylor. Wilkinson could only recommend them for $500; they favored separation "but have not carried their views further." Members of the fourth category, a miscellaneous group, acted "without concert or Union" and were enemies of the general plan, but they had to be considered. George Nicholas was valued at $2,000, apostate George Muter at $1,200, and General Lawson, Alexander Scott Bullitt, Thomas Marshall, and Robert C. Anderson at $1,000 each. Samuel Taylor, Green Clay, and Robert Caldwell were put down for $500, and Humphrey Marshall, "a Villain of no principle" who could be "very troublesome." was listed at $600.[15] Membership on this roll of bribeables resulted in considerable embarrassment for a number of politicians when its contents were later revealed.

Miro responded favorably to the request for funds, although the granting of royal pensions was beyond his powers, and on September 19, the day Wilkinson started on his overland trek home, Miro supplied the Kentuckian with $7,000 in silver. It was to be considered a loan if the pension was not granted. The governor recommended to his government that Wilkinson receive 2,000 pesos a year and be given a military rank suitable for his services and abilities. His wife should be given a 1,000-peso pension after his death if his goals had been attained.

Wilkinson returned overland from New Orleans as far as Nashville, where he took boat for Louisville. Although delayed in Natchez by illness, he was with his family by mid-December. Despite Miro's donation, Wilkinson's economic condition was deteriorating. His near monopoly of the Mississippi trade had been destroyed when Spain opened it to anyone who paid a tax on the goods carried, and Wilkinson had suffered some severe operating losses through lost boats and damaged and inferior cargo. During his stay in New Orleans he had dissolved his partnership with Daniel Clark, who had handled the New Orleans end of the business.[16]

When Wilkinson learned of the decisions of the Eighth Convention and passage of the Fourth Enabling Act, he must have realized that if there had ever been a chance of detaching Kentucky from the Union and attaching it to Spain, that chance was gone. His commercial prospects were declining, and his lavish expenses were carrying him ever nearer to economic disaster. Yet he still hoped that fortune would turn his way. Perhaps he could continue to milk the Spanish connection. Perhaps Miro could be persuaded to advance other sums, perhaps the king would grant the pension. As Kentucky moved ever closer to statehood in the Union, Wilkinson continued to cultivate his Spanish contacts. He tried to impress Spanish officials with the value of the information he supplied and the accuracy of his predictions that something might yet be done to advance Spanish interests in the Mississippi Valley. He pretended to cooperate with Dr. James O'Fallon and the South Carolina-Yazoo Land Company colonization scheme, but he kept Miro informed of what was happening so that the scheme could be crushed at the right moment.[17]

When Miro at last received an answer from officials in Spain to his recommendations concerning Wilkinson, they

were negative. Wilkinson was not to be granted a commission
or pension, and Miro was forbidden to give money to promote
a revolution in Kentucky or to deal with Kentucky unless it had
established its independence from the United States. By now,
such approaches would have had little chance for success, in
any case. Much of the District's unhappiness with Spain had
been eased by the opening of the Mississippi to general trade
and the encouragement of immigration into Spanish territory
on what appeared to be liberal terms. All of this was unsatisfactory as a permanent solution, but it would serve for the time.
As tensions eased, the potential for discontent that would
provoke Kentuckians into taking drastic action faded into
near fantasy. Rumors continued to circulate about Wilkinson's
Spanish dealings, and they were no longer greeted with the
approval they had earlier received from many westerners.
Followers began to ease away from Wilkinson, until he declared that only Sebastian remained loyal to him. It was time
to move on.

Wilkinson refused to seek election to the Ninth Convention, and he left Kentucky in 1791, leaving Harry Innes to close
his tangled accounts. Aided by strong recommendations from
John Brown and George Nicholas, Wilkinson managed to secure an army commission in October 1791. Although he
blamed the inaction of the Spanish government for the failure
of his grand scheme, Wilkinson carefully preserved his association with the Louisiana administrators. Conditions might
change in his favor, and his fertile imagination might devise
some way to profit from the association.[18]

With Wilkinson in an inactive role and most of his adherents deserting him, the Ninth Convention completed its
work quickly. The general public indicated little interest in its
meeting. Conventions had become commonplace by 1790, and
people had other more pressing concerns. When the convention met on Monday, July 26, 1790, in Danville, the court
faction was notably missing. Even Samuel McDowell, who had
presided over all the conventions except the first, was absent.
George Muter replaced him in the chair, and Thomas Todd
continued as clerk. Isaac Shelby and Benjamin Logan were the

only acknowledged members of the court party, and they were not members of what had been the hard core of that faction. Rules of the last convention were adopted, and the usual committees were appointed. A copy of the United States Constitution was ordered to lie on the clerk's table for easy reference. The housekeeping chores completed, the convention went into committee-of-the-whole, with James Garrard in the chair, to consider the Fourth Enabling Act. Later that day the committee requested and received permission to continue its deliberations on Tuesday.[19]

Several latecomers on Tuesday morning encountered an unusually conscientious Committee on Privileges and Elections. Chairman Thomas Allin reported favorably on the election returns from Jefferson, Madison, Nelson, Fayette, Monroe, Woodford, and Mason counties, but he said that no general returns had been submitted for Bourbon and Lincoln. Since they appeared to have been duly elected, however, the committee recommended the seating of Benjamin Logan, William Montgomery, John Bryan, James Davis, James Garrard, and a Mr. Shipp. The rest of the day's work was done in committee-of-the-whole. Some progress was reported, but the committee received permission to continue its labors on Wednesday.[20]

On Wednesday the convention assembled at nine o'clock, an hour earlier than usual. The missing general returns from Bourbon and Lincoln counties had arrived, and lingering doubts about the legality of some delegates were resolved. Nicholas Lewis was appointed sergeant-at-arms, a position apparently not used in the earlier conventions, and one of the standing rules was modified. Then, with Allin presiding, the convention again turned itself into the committee-of-the-whole. Later that day Allin reported a resolution that requested separation: "Resolved, That it is expedient for, and the will of the good people of the District of Kentucky that the same be erected into an Independent State, on the terms and conditions specified in an Act of the Virginia Assembly passed the 18th day of December, 1789 entitled an Act concerning the erection of the District of Kentucky into an Independent State." Someone called for a recorded vote, and the resolution was adopted by the surprisingly narrow margin of 24 to 18. Shelby and Logan joined the members of the country faction to make the majority. For the fifth time, representatives of the citizens of Kentucky had requested separation and statehood.

The delegates then agreed on June 1, 1792, as the date when "the said District of Kentucky shall become a State separate from & independent of the Government of Virginia and that the said articles become a Solemn compact binding on the said People." A select committee of eleven members was given until the following day to draft addresses to the Virginia General Assembly and Congress notifying them of the decision and, in the case of Congress, requesting an act of admission.[21]

The committee had completed its assignment by Thursday morning, and Bullitt opened the session by introducing the address to the Virginia House of Representatives. Pertinent portions of the journal were attached to show both the renewed request for statehood and the date selected for the final detachment. "We cannot signify thus our determination," the address added gracefully, "without feeling & expressing the warmest gratitude for your constant and unwearied attention to our Interest, & your uninterrupted indulgence to us in all our wishes." Kentucky hoped that the friendship shown heretofore would continue in the future.

James Marshall, a son of Thomas Marshall, then moved that the necessary steps be taken to provide for the meeting of a constitutional convention. His resolution was directed to the committee-of-the-whole. Later in the day committee chairman James Garrard reported that the committee had some amendments to propose, but the convention decided to postpone consideration of them until the following day, Friday, July 30. Earlier in the day, when the committee-of-the-whole was working on the address to Congress, it asked permission to carry its work over into Friday. Such requests were usually routinely granted, but upon this occasion a select committee of six members was appointed to continue the drafting of a suitable address.[22] No reason was given for this action, but a majority of the members must have been dissatisfied with the progress being made in the large committee.

The Ninth Convention completed its session on a busy Friday. Business started with James Marshall reporting the select committee's address to Congress. That necessitated another conversion into the committee-of-the-whole. When the convention reconvened, James Garrard read the proposed address "To the President and the Honble. the Congress of the United States." To assuage any doubts about the loyalty of Kentuckians, it declared that the inhabitants of Kentucky were "as firmly attached to the happy establishment of the Federal Government as any of the Citizens of the United States." Despite great hazards and much difficulty, the District had grown so that "At this day, the population and strength of the Country renders it fully able, in the Opinion of your Memorialists, to form and support an efficient domestic Government." This growth had increased the inconvenience of being a distant part of Virginia, but the memorialists were grateful to Virginia for supporting their request for statehood. They asked the president and Congress to sanction their separation before November 1, 1791. Then Kentucky could hold a constitutional convention between that date and June 1, 1792, when they hoped to become a member of the Union.

Garrard then presented the committee report on the holding of a constitutional convention. As amended, the measure called for the election of five delegates from each county at the December 1791 court days. Eligible to vote were free white males above age twenty-one who had resided in Kentucky for at least one year. A certificate of election was to be given each successful candidate, and the results in each county were to be reported to the clerk of the District's Supreme Court, who would present them to the convention when it convened. Officers who did not comply with these provisions could be sued by anyone for £100. The convention, to meet in Danville on the first Monday in April 1792, was charged "to frame and establish a Constitution or form of Government for the good people of Kentucky." It was also to decide what Virginia laws would remain in force until the legislature of the new state had time to act. To provide for a possible emergency meeting, the president of the Ninth Convention, "with the advice of three or upon the request of five members," or, in the case of the death or disability of the president, any six members of the Ninth Convention, could convene the convention. The clerk was ordered to send copies of the separation documents to the president and Congress, and the editor of the *Kentucky Gazette* was requested to publish the proceedings of the Ninth Convention in two successive issues. Its work completed, the convention adjourned until May 20, 1791.[23]

The departing delegates had little apprehension about receiving the approval of the federal government, and their confidence was well founded. In his annual message to Congress on December 8, 1790, President Washington included a strong recommendation that Kentucky be admitted into the Union. He asserted that "the liberality and harmony" of the negotiations honored both parties, and "the sentiments of warm attachment to the Union and its present Government expressed by our fellow-citizens of Kentucky can not fail to add an affectionate concern for their particular welfare." In their replies to his message, both houses of Congress endorsed the president's recommendation. Congress completed passage of the admission act on February 4, 1791, and Washington signed it. The earlier opposition of some northerners to Kentucky's admission had been relieved by Vermont's request for statehood, which was also moving toward acceptance. A contemporary jingle reflected the early concern for sectional balance:

> Kentucky to the Union given,
> Vermont will make the balance even,
> Still Pennsylvania holds the scales,
> And neither South nor North prevails.

The bill admitting Vermont passed some two weeks after the Kentucky measure, but Vermont's date of admission was set at March 4, 1791, while the act for Kentucky accepted the June 1, 1792, date specified in the Virginia compact.[24] The fates that had caused so many delays in Kentucky's separation movement seemed determined to inflict one last prolongation on the long admission process.

The census of 1790 gave startling proof of Kentucky's population readiness for statehood. The Northwest Ordinance of
1787 had set at 60,000 the number of free inhabitants required
for statehood in that region, and that number was generally
accepted as a standard elsewhere, although the "free inhabitants" requirement could cause dispute in a slave state where
the Federal Constitution called for five slaves to be counted as
equal to three free persons. In 1790 the District of Kentucky
was reported to have 73,677 inhabitants, including 12,430
slaves. The inclusive figure was some 4,000 more than the
population of Rhode Island. This was an amazing increase in
the fifteen years since a few score pioneers had struggled for
survival in a handful of isolated stations. The free white males
aged sixteen and up numbered 15,154; the free white males
under sixteen numbered 17,057. The 28,922 white females (of
all ages) constituted 47.3 percent of the white population. The
slave population had also increased rapidly, and the 12,430
persons held in bondage made up 16.8 percent of the population. "All other free persons" numbered only 114, and most of
them were probably free blacks. The great majority of Kentuckians of 1790 were native-born Americans; none of the early
leaders in the District had been born outside North America.

Settlers were continuing to pour into Kentucky, although
travel was still difficult and dangerous. Wheeled vehicles had
still not conquered Cumberland Gap, and the Ohio River still
had its navigational problems. Indians remained a danger on
both routes as well as within the interior of the District, although the day of large raids was past. George Thompson said
that on March 21, 1790, Indians had attacked the boats on
which he was descending the river. They were driven off after a
three-hour battle, but the defenders lost two of their unwieldy
vessels and property worth an estimated £2,500. When he
returned east through Cumberland Gap, Thompson's party
lost a man to the Indians there. The *Kentucky Gazette* of May 3,
1790, carried an announcement that a large party bound for
the east would depart Crab Orchard on May 25 for the passage
through the Cumberland Gap.[25] The ineffective efforts of the
federal government to curb the Indians exacerbated the Kentuckians' discontent.

Yet everywhere, the land revealed signs of substantial progress. Thousands of acres were being cleared, and stumps were being removed from the early fields that had been cleared "Kentucky style." Some of the first crude cabins were being replaced by larger and more comfortable homes, including some of brick and stone. Large game had almost disappeared from vast areas of Kentucky, and broadcloth was seen more often than buckskins on the town streets. The advertisements in the *Kentucky Gazette* revealed a rapid increase in the number and variety of business establishments. Specialty shops, such as that of a silversmith, were competing for trade with the several general stores. Small manufacturing establishments were getting started, and the Kentucky Society for Promoting Manufactures had been organized in 1789. A year earlier a number of residents had pledged to use domestic products instead of foreign luxuries. Commerce was increasing, and the growing use of keelboats increased the expensive upstream traffic. Other towns were also growing, but Lexington, with 835 inhabitants in 1790, was a regional center of increasing importance. Around the new log jail was a painted black stripe that showed the expanded limits for debtors; civilization had come to the Kentucky frontier.

Yet, as historian Joan Coward has written of this period, "Kentucky remained an inchoate society" with limited political institutions and experiences and a residue of political bitterness.[26] The society was still new, it had not had time to season, to mature, and its thin fabric could be easily rent. On the eve of statehood, one might wonder if the District of Kentucky was capable of framing a constitution. Could the leaders of a new state translate a document into a viable government? Such questions had not been answered when the Ninth Convention adjourned.

FIVE

Writing the Constitution

The issue of separation was settled, with little dissention remaining, when the Ninth Convention completed its work. Most Virginians in the District of Kentucky had realized that someday Kentucky would sever its ties with the Old Dominion; the pertinent questions had been when and on what terms. Independence from the United States and a possible association with Spain had never had mass appeal, and the agreement reached in the summer of 1790 was approved by most inhabitants of the District. The terms of separation had been approved by the convention, by Virginia, and by the United States, and on June 1, 1792, Kentucky would enter the Union as a state—provided it had a constitution by then. The dominant issue was no longer separation but the nature of the government the Tenth Convention would provide for the new state. On that issue, Kentuckians displayed considerable concern and disagreement.

Many Kentuckians were concerned that the District might not have men capable of writing an acceptable constitution. While much of the area was passing rapidly beyond the frontier stage, Kentucky lacked the political stability and experience that was so prevalent in eastern Virginia and other long established communities. The Old Dominion had a strong political infrastructure with well established institutions and a large cadre of men who were accustomed to governing and managing affairs on various levels. Call a convention in Virginia, such as the 1788 ratifying convention, and one could be sure that a number of respected leaders would participate actively in the decisionmaking. Thomas Jefferson, James Madison, Patrick Henry, George Mason, George Wythe, and a score of others constituted an exceptional reservoir of political talent. Such a resource had not yet collected in Kentucky. Few Kentuckians had experienced extended service in even the General Assembly; election to that body was more often evaded than sought. The District's delegates to the 1788 ratifying convention may have been keen observers, but they played no part in the deliberations of that body. Only John Brown had limited experience in the national Congress. Few members of the Tenth Convention had extensive experience that would be helpful in making a constitution.[1]

Some of the Kentuckians who belonged to the class from which leadership was most likely to come were skeptical of their ability to provide a satisfactory form of government. "I hope the deliberations of the Kentucky Convention will terminate more favorably than you seem to apprehend," John Brown wrote Harry Innes, "'tho I must confess that your communications upon the subject added to what I had before collected relative to the political sentiments of many of the members have excited in my mind serious apprehensions, that the result of their labors may fall greatly short of the public expectation." Then with great prescience Brown expressed his fear of an attitude that would hamper the Commonwealth for most of its first two centuries: "It would be a circumstance truly humiliating, if at this day when the subject of Government is so fully understood, Kentucky actuated by motives of niggardly economy, should adopt a bad form of Government rather than incur the necessary expenses of a good one." Hubbard Taylor, a member of the Tenth Convention, remained concerned after the constitution was drafted and the day of statehood neared. As he told James Madison, he was uneasy about starting the government, "not so much on account of a disposition to act contrary to the interests of the Community, as for the real want of Capacity to do things in a regular, proper & equitable manner." The problem, he complained, was "our want of men of Abilities, in this Country."[2]

If there was doubt about the ability of Kentuckians to write a constitution, a possible solution was to seek outside assistance. None of the conventions made a plea for help, but several individuals tried to obtain assistance from such eastern Virginians as Thomas Jefferson, George Nicholas, and Edmund Pendleton. But as usual when help was needed, Kentuckians placed most of their trust in James Madison. At least four men tried to enlist his aid in the making of the constitution. One of them assured Madison that if he would draft the document "there is every reason to believe that it would be adopted in toto." Madison refused to become the draftsman, but twice he explained in some detail the features he believed should be in a good state constitution. Among his recommendations were: a powerful upper house in the legislature with its members elected to six-year terms by voters who met a property-holding qualification; a strong system of separation of powers among the three branches of government; a lower house whose members were elected annually without the property-holding qualification for voters; a president who would be assisted (and checked) by a council of state chosen by the voters; and judges, appointed by the executive and legislature, with good salaries and life tenure during good behavior.[3] Although generous with his ideas, Madison would not go beyond that point in constitution making; Kentuckians would have to write their own document.

If they lacked experience in constitution making and legislative service, a number of Kentuckians had at least given considerable thought to constitutional issues over a number of years. The form of government for an independent Kentucky became a matter for serious consideration as soon as separation from Virginia became a possibility. That interest increased after the District began holding its interminable series of conventions. The most comprehensive study of what a constitution should contain was made by the Danville Political Club. In addition to studying and debating about separation, the club in early 1787 set up a committee to prepare a constitution and a bill of rights. The club's incomplete records do not contain the results of these labors, but in various meetings the members decided that: representation should be by population, not by county; annual elections were best for a free government; voting should be restricted by some qualification other than age and freedom; the legislature should consist of two houses; the constitution should be superior to an act of the legislature; and the president and members of the upper house should be allowed to succeed themselves. The club also saw the need for a "Declaration of Rights" to precede the United States Constitution; presumably such a document was needed on the state level as well. The theme running through the recommendations was the need to provide protection from a possible tyrannical government. As Harry Innes put it, "Ninety-nine men out of a hundred possessed of power will abuse it." A good government would limit the chances for such abuse. Since several members of the Danville Political Club served in subsequent conventions, the club's recommendations were in a position to exert some influence on the decisions made. The historian of the club argued that its members received far too little credit for the writing of the state's first constitution. "The demands of the hour," he asserted, "were met in the Political Club."[4]

Most historians who have studied the convention era have disagreed with that assertion. Then and now, George Nicholas has been hailed as "the father of the 1792 constitution," despite his determination to remain aloof from the politics of his new home. In 1789, when Thomas Marshall urged him to seek election to the Eighth Convention, Nicholas replied that "my observations since I got here have confirmed the resolution not to engage in politics again." He could contribute little, Nicholas explained, because he would have to cast his vote on important issues before he could become "intimately acquainted" with the District's political situation. Besides, he confessed, political involvement would affect his private affairs. He had a strong regard for the welfare of the country in which he had decided to live, but "nothing but a crisis which shall appear to me to threaten the ruin of the country and make it disgraceful to remain silent will induce me again to take a place in the political line." Two years later he brushed off Madison's suggestion that he should be in Congress, but in

1792 Nicholas sought and won election to the Tenth Convention. Perhaps he decided that there was a crisis; perhaps he also doubted the quality of available leadership; or perhaps he was a political animal who could not long resist the lure of politics. Nicholas had definite ideas on the features a good government should have, and he wanted Kentucky's first independent government to be one under which he and the state could prosper. Once Nicholas decided to participate, he began careful preparation for the dominant role he was to play in the 1792 convention.[5] In some respects his role there was similar to James Madison's role in the federal convention of 1787. Unfortunately, Nicholas did not take copious notes on the daily deliberations.

Increased attention was devoted to the form the new government would take once it became evident that statehood was certain. Taverns must have witnessed informal discussions, and interested Kentuckians wherever they met must have argued over some of the controversial points. Some private letters discussed the writer's views or asked the opinion of the recipient, but with two exceptions the contemporary records reveal little about the constitutional discussions. The pages of the *Kentucky Gazette* not filled with advertisements were packed with letters to the editor, and most of them dealt with the forthcoming constitutional convention and what it should do. The second exception, which also appeared in Bradford's newspaper, consisted of the activities of county committees, formed by members of the partisan faction, which sought to control the convention by electing instructed delegates to it. In 1788 the partisans had wanted to ascertain the views of the people by polling the members of the militia companies. That attempt failed, but after the adjournment of the Ninth Convention they resurrected the idea in an effort to shape the constitution to their interests and desires. County committees were formed in at least five counties (Bourbon, Fayette, Madison, Mason, and Mercer), and may have existed in the others as well. Overall coordination proved difficult. When the Fayette committee called for a meeting of county delegates at Harrodsburg, only three county committees responded.

The Bourbon County committee was more active and left more records of its activities than any of the others. This group started with the premise that all power rested with the people, whose desires could be known only by means of annual elections of their representatives or through committees elected by the people. In Bourbon County each militia company sent two delegates to a county committee, which then nominated a slate of candidates for the constitutional convention. The names of the nominees were returned to the militia company committees, which could make changes before returning them to the county committee. The Bourbon County committee hoped this democratic procedure would forestall most of the "disorder and confusion" that usually prevailed at elections. "Our liberty cost us much blood and treasure," the committee asserted, "and we were brave enough to support it, when invaded by an enemy which is a terror of all Europe; let us also be wise enough now, not in any measure to be unheeded out of our just rights, by flattery, grog, or the wag of a ruffled hand."

This county committee drew up some general instructions for the Bourbon County delegates; through the agency of the *Kentucky Gazette* it submitted them to the "serious consideration" of citizens elsewhere. The legislature should consist of one house. Immoral men should be excluded from office. The people should elect directly most civil officials and militia officers from the rank of colonel down. Voting should be by ballot, not by voice. Kentucky should not use the laws of England or any other country or state. Instead, "a simple, and concise code of laws [should] be framed, adapted to the weakest capacity: which we humbly believe, will happily supercede the necessity of attorneys, pleading in our state." All land and other forms of property should be subject to taxation.[6]

These suggestions and the advocacy of instructed delegates elicited protests which the proponents answered in the *Kentucky Gazette* of October 22, 1791. True, no law authorized the use of county committees, but no law prohibited their use. The people had the right to assemble peaceably to make known their views, and committees had been important during the movement toward national independence. Opponents charged that such committees would create factions within the state, but committees had promoted unity during the Revolutionary era, and that could also be true during Kentucky's transition to statehood. Some critics had claimed that delegates would be degraded if they were given instructions; but if you hired someone to build a house, wouldn't you tell him what you wanted?[7]

The partisans obviously considered elections a key to the type of government they desired, and one John Boyd sent editor Bradford the Bourbon County committee's recommendations on that vital point. The partisans wanted to divide the county into "districts" with approximately 200 freemen in each. The only suffrage requirements would be free, white, male, twenty-one years of age, and residence in the county for one year and in the district for six months. On the first Tuesday in March the freemen of a district would elect three "registrars," who would maintain a list of the district's freemen. Any two registrars or any three freemen could assemble all of the freemen in the district to consult for the common good. The registrars in each county would meet at least once a year to consider matters of common interest, to instruct the representatives of the people, and to present requests to the legislature. On the second Tuesday in August, upon the call of the registrars, the freemen would assemble and by ballot elect county and other officials. All civil elections would be by ballot.[8] These proposals for participatory democracy went well beyond what Kentuckians were accustomed to in government; they exceeded the democratic limits that the majority of Kentuckians were willing to accept at that time.

Most of the committee recommendations were doomed to fail, but they started a lively debate in the pages of the *Kentucky Gazette* during the interval between the Ninth Convention and the Tenth. Harry Innes scoffed at the pretensions of the peasantry, with their extraordinary prejudices, who wanted *"plain honest Farmers"* to make the constitution. The outcome of the campaign was still uncertain, Innes proclaimed, but "they have given a very serious alarm to every thinking man, who are determined to watch and count the temper of the people." The delegates to the convention were aware of the temper of the times, and the agitation by the partisan faction may well have kept the constitution from being more conservative than it was.

The issues discussed and the recommendations made took many forms, as the columns of the *Kentucky Gazette* revealed. "A.B.C." argued for separation of powers but denied that the government should be run by all the people; some were more capable than others. He hoped the most able men in the District would be sent to the constitutional convention, and he warned against including provisions in the constitution that would have to be violated at times on behalf of the general welfare. "Will Wisp" retorted that "these great men will always out talk us and out dispute us"; they should not be trusted to make the constitution. When it came to government, he declared, the common people could run it at one-tenth the cost of great-man rule. "Felte Firebrand" penned a sarcastic response to the Bourbon County committee. In its work he detected an attempt by a few to dictate to the mass of the people, and he charged that the committees of the 1770s had committed many acts of tyranny and injustice. The claim that an inexpensive government was possible simply was not true.

"A Medlar," who identified herself as a woman, endorsed the partisans' objection to letting "great men" draft the constitution. She had found the "most solid wisdom among those who live above poverty and yet below affluence." If the author was indeed a female, her entry into Kentucky political discussion on the public level may have been a first for women in the District. "H.S.B.M." attacked the aristocratic stance of "A.B.C.," who had rejected the concept of committees without waiting to see what they did when they met. Instead of ignoring the popular committees, he wanted them to have the power to veto acts of the legislature. He also hoped lawyers would be excluded from the legislature so that state laws would be simple and understandable. Several partisans echoed his apprehension of having attorneys involved in the constitutional and legislative processes, but few matched the directness of "Salamander," who proclaimed that "the fewer Lawyers and

Pick pockets there are in a country, the better the chance honest people have to keep their own."[9]

And the debate continued. "Philip Philips," a recent comer to Mercer County, injected an antislavery note that must have astounded many of his readers. Being antislavery was not uncommon, but the author asserted that if blacks were educated as much as whites, little difference would be found in the mental capacities of the two races. He predicted the end of slavery at some future date. "H.S.B.M." had earlier declared that blacks were a part of the human race and were therefore covered by protection of any bill of rights, but he was unable to accept the idea of racial equality. "Little Brutus" responded quickly to assaults against the institution of slavery. He defended the right of an owner both to hold slaves and to free them if he saw fit to do so. "Brutus Senior" waited for two months before replying to "Little Brutus." No one had the right to hold stolen property, and that, he asserted, was the true status of slavery. He denied the assertions that the end of slavery would injure the economy and retard Kentucky's growth. True, he admitted, the blacks "are destitute of property, have a natural propensity to idleness, [are] void of religion, education, honor, honesty, understanding, gratitude, etc." But "All this is a necessary and unavoidable consequence of slavery. . . . A stronger argument could not be brought against it."

"A.B.C." responded to the criticism of his previous effort by "A Medlar" and "H.S.B.M." He doubted that the former was a woman, since the writing lacked "a certain delicacy and benevolence one finds in the fair sex." But if the author was actually a female, he referred her to St. Paul's comments on busybodies. He suspected that his other critic was the great champion of the Bourbon County committee. "A.B.C." charged that the delegates selected by that committee would not adequately represent the will of the people, since a small group would dictate the choice. The constitution should be framed by delegates of the people, not by men who had been instructed by a committee. "A Citizen" joined in the denunciation of the county committees. "Have you my fellow Country men," he

inquired, "resigned your rights as Freemen and Electors?"
Surely they could judge of the qualifications of prospective
delegates to the convention without being assisted by "some
more gifted minds." As he viewed the situation, the question
was "whether we will give our unbiased votes as becomes Free
men, or submit to have our choice directed by Committees and
vote only as they shall direct." His position was endorsed by
"X.Y.Z.," who was convinced that "giving instructions to representatives is the most vague and unformed privilege which was
ever claimed; and that any thing of a public nature not done
agreeable to some established rule, is arbitrary and dangerous
to liberty." [10]

The most extensive discussion of the form the state government should take came from the busy pen of "The Disinterested Citizen," who was probably George Nicholas. The
ideas expressed in the series of letters in the *Kentucky Gazette*
closely resembled the points Nicholas advocated in the April
1792 convention. The author of the letters stressed the need for
a constitution as a way "to restrain the exercise of delegated
powers," for citizens could not be secure "without imposing
restrictions upon our rulers." Human nature being what it
was, precautions were necessary "to prevent a sacrifice of the
interests of the many to the few." Since any class of men would,
if possible, take advantage of the rest, the different classes
must be represented in the government, each helping check
the others. In addition to the constitution itself, a bill of rights
was needed to prevent possible abuses of power. It could be
incorporated in the constitution, although it usually stood
alone. "Disinterested Citizen" also stressed the need for separation of powers and a system of checks and balances among
the branches of government. Unless this was done, he predicted that the legislature would dominate the other branches,
as it had in Virginia. While the people must be free to elect
their representatives, a strong upper house was needed to
check the unstable tendencies of the lower house. Some sort of
property qualification should be required before one could
vote for the members of the upper house. [11]

Such advocates presented a bewildering welter of suggestions during the months before the 1792 convention, but most of them centered around three major questions: Who should be entrusted to write the constitution, and should they accept instructions from the county committees? What type of government should be established and how democratic should it be? What should be the future of slavery in the new state?

The importance of the work of the convention and the activities of the county committees produced a more hotly contested election than had been true for most of the earlier conventions. George Nicholas was only one of the "great men" who was forced to campaign more actively than he had intended in order to secure election. When the forty-five delegates had been elected, five from each of the nine counties, it was difficult to tell which of the warring factions had been most successful. While such well known figures as Benjamin Sebastian, James Garrard, George Nicholas, Samuel McDowell, Benjamin Logan, Isaac Shelby and Caleb Wallace won seats, other prominent individuals had been left at home. No member of the Marshall clan had been elected, John Brown was not there, James Wilkinson had left the state, Harry Innes did not become a delegate until a vacancy occurred after the convention was underway. Humphrey Marshall, piqued by his exclusion, sniffed that the convention "drew forth as members, those who had taken most pains to please, or who happened at the time, to be, the greatest favorites of the people." A slight majority of the members might be identified with the partisan faction; Samuel Taylor, the perennial conventioneer, was their chief spokesman.

Most of the delegates, including the partisans, were men of some substance. Nearly all owned land, most of them paid taxes on cattle and horses, and two-thirds of them owned at least five slaves. Active ministers had been absent from the earlier conventions, but seven (three Presbyterians, three Baptists and a Methodist) held seats in 1792. They were all antislavery to some degree, and they probably sought election in the hope of inserting antislavery provisions in the constitution. The public's distrust of lawyers limited the bar's representation to George Nicholas and Benjamin Sebastian. Incomplete

biographies indicate that no more than six had attended college, that at least one-third had no previous experience in
either conventions or legislative bodies. Such experience was
sharply limited for most of the others by both duration and
active participation.[12] The lack of experience was one of the
most evident characteristics of the group.

This paucity of experience, and possibly talent, could have
been disastrous had Nicholas not been a member of the convention. He was the best qualified member to direct its work,
and once he decided to come out of his self-imposed political
exile he did not stint his efforts to secure a satisfactory document. "Old Nick" was familiar with the Pennsylvania constitution of 1776 which, written by the likes of Kentucky's
partisans, had been the most radical democratic constitution
of the Revolutionary era. In 1790 another convention had re-
written the 1776 document along more conservative lines, and
Nicholas was determined to keep Kentucky from undergoing
the Quaker state's experience. He was also very familiar with
both the Virginia and federal constitutions. Nicholas went to
the Tenth Convention armed with that determination, his skill
as a debater, his reputation as being the best lawyer in Kentucky and well formulated ideas on what form the constitution
should take.

The opening of the Tenth Convention in Danville on Monday, April 2, 1792 resembled closely the opening sessions of
the recent conventions. The setting was the same, Samuel
McDowell was again elected to preside, Thomas Todd was
again appointed clerk, the rules of the July 1789 convention
were adopted. George Muter, president of the Ninth Convention, had sent a letter with enclosures; the Fourth Enabling Act
and its acceptance by the Ninth Convention were read and
ordered sent to the committee-of-the-whole in which the convention conducted most of its deliberations. Nine members,
headed by Nicholas, were appointed to the Committee on
Privileges and Ethics, and Joshua Barbee was made sergeant-
at-arms and Roger Devine became the doorkeeper. When the
first day's routine business was completed the convention adjourned until ten o'clock Tuesday morning, when it would
meet in the Presbyterian meeting house.[13]

On Tuesday morning the convention received some partisan petitions from Bourbon County; they were read and sent to the committee-of-the-whole. The convention then went into committee with James Garrard in the chair. The committee kept no record of its discussions except for formal motions presented to the convention, but Nicholas apparently opened its deliberations by delivering a long and carefully prepared address. He emphasized the need for a spirit of cooperation so that they could write a constitution that met the needs of the people. It would not be perfect, he warned, but it should protect individual rights while creating a government with ample power to protect the interests of the state. Concentrated power was dangerous, so he advocated a careful separation of powers among the branches of government. Frequent changes in legislative personnel would also promote safety, for it would hamper the formation of party combinations that would violate the purpose of separation of powers. When the committee reported some progress to the convention it received permission to sit again on Wednesday.[14]

The convention continued to do most of its work in committee during the next several days. Garrard chaired the committee on Wednesday; Isaac Shelby occupied that position on Thursday, Friday and Saturday, April 5-7. Each day the chairman rendered the same report, some progress had been made, and permission was requested to meet again at the following session. Clerk Todd made only brief and almost identical entries except for changing the dates. Only tantalizing scraps of information hint at what occurred in the committee sessions; even the dates of major speeches and debates are uncertain. George Nicholas was the key figure. While he did not bring a draft of a constitution to the convention, he had worked carefully on the points he believed the final documents should contain, and there is no doubt but that he was the best prepared member of the convention. His proposals formed the basis for discussion.

It was probably on Wednesday, April 4, that Nicholas spent considerable time defending the concept of a two house legislature against the partisan demand for a democratic one house body. Nicholas contended that having only one house would result in a dangerous concentration of power. He agreed that the lower house should have frequent elections with few restrictions on membership so that it would be responsible to the people, but he argued successfully that as a check there should be an upper house whose members would have higher qualifications and would serve longer terms. He tried to reduce the spirit of localism by having senators elected on a state wide basis, but he was not able to convince a majority of the delegates of the value of that proposal.

Thursday's discussion centered on the issue of suffrage, and Nicholas probably surprised some of his more radical opponents by agreeing that all free male citizens of legal age should be allowed to vote. The nature of a government, he asserted, depended upon the suffrage. If only a few could vote, it would be aristocratic; if all could vote, it was republican. Even this proposal, radical in the context of its times, did not venture to suggest that the right to vote should also include white women and free blacks, much less slaves. Even radicalism had its limits.

Nicholas apparently used part of Friday to direct the committee's attention to the office of governor. True to his belief in the separation of powers, he advocated a strong executive who could make appointments and veto legislation, and he opposed the idea of an executive council which would dilute the powers of the governor. In another partisan type proposal, Nicholas called for the governor to be elected by direct popular vote. He insisted that the voters were capable of selecting the natural leader who stood out from the crowd, and he was willing to trust them to do so. Popular election, Nicholas argued, would reduce the danger of bribery, corruption and factionalism. The governor's salary must be large enough for a man to accept the position without having other financial resources. Direct election was too radical for a majority of the members, and Nicholas was defeated on that issue.[15]

Sharp differences also emerged on Saturday when the committee-of-the-whole directed its attention to the judiciary. Most partisans were convinced that lawyers were venal and an unnecessary evil; they used their devious training chiefly to deprive honest men of their lands. Therefore, the entire legal system should be curbed as much as possible to prevent abuses. Lawyer Nicholas defended the legal system as a bulwark that protected the constitution and the bill of rights. True liberty, he maintained, could only be attained and retained through a just application of the laws, and that was impossible without courts, judges and lawyers. He advocated a system of courts, adequate in number and with frequent sessions, headed by a Supreme Court that would provide uniformity for the system through its appellate jurisdiction. Judges, appointed by the governor, should have their independence protected by fixed salaries and indefinite terms. But to prevent judicial abuse, judges should be subject to impeachment or to removal by the governor upon the request of two-thirds of both houses of the legislature.

Several delegates dissented sharply from Nicholas' plans for the judiciary. The most controversial point concerned his proposed solution to the endless land cases that made up most of the docket in the District's courts. Nicholas proposed to end the long drawn out controversies by giving the state's Supreme Court original and final jurisdiction in land litigation cases. The partisans objected at once; what he proposed was just an even quicker way to take their land away from the poor. Other members must also have been concerned over the drastic change in the judicial process that would eliminate the possibility of appeal in the majority of Kentucky court cases.

Some time on Saturday Nicholas resigned his seat in a letter that gave no explanation for the unusual step. The explanation generally accepted is that he had not discussed the proposed original jurisdiction of the Supreme Court during the election for delegates, and, in view of the opposition to it in the committee, he could not be sure that he had the support of the Mercer County voters who had elected him. The convention immediately issued a writ of election to fill the unexpected vacancy and voted its thanks to Nicholas for his contributions to its work. The voters who appeared at the Mercer County courthouse on Monday, April 9, presumably heard Nicholas defend his position. They then re-elected him to the constitutional convention. The convention did not meet on Monday, the journal reported because of inclement weather. But several members may have stayed away to prevent the formation of a quorum so that Nicholas, whose re-election they anticipated, would not miss any of the sessions. He returned on Tuesday, strengthened by a fresh mandate from the people, and resumed his leadership of the committee's work.[16]

Garrard chaired the committee on Tuesday and Wednesday as work continued in the committee-of-the-whole. Another resignation was submitted by a leading delegate on Wednesday, April 11. The Reverend David Rice, a Presbyterian minister from Mercer County who led the antislavery group, also resigned without providing a reason. Known as "Father Rice," he had become a minister after graduating from Princeton in 1761. He was not favorably impressed by the District's land disputes when he visited Kentucky in 1783, and he prepared to return to the east. But he had deeply impressed those who had met and heard him, and he agreed to remain to preach when over 300 people signed the strict covenant which he drew up. Rice established several churches, taught school, and became chairman of the board of what became Transylvania Seminary. In 1786 he was elected first moderator of the Presbytery, and in 1792 his popularity sent him to the convention as one of the leading advocates of opposition to slavery.

Slavery had existed in Kentucky from the early days of settlement, and by 1792 some 22.8% of the white householders held slaves. The percentage ranged from 12.6 in Mason County to 35.3 in Woodford. The average Kentucky slaveholder in 1792 held 4.32 slaves. Antislavery sentiment had also existed in Kentucky from the early days of settlement with much of its strength centered in some of the churches. Opponents of the institution, who hoped to curb it in Kentucky before it became too firmly fixed in the economy and society, fixed their hopes upon the constitutional convention. Few Kentuckians were abolitionists who demanded the immediate end of slavery without compensation to the masters. Most of the antislavery advocates accepted the legality of slavery under state and national law; indeed, several of the leading opponents of slavery in Kentucky, including Father Rice, were slaveholders. Antislavery took many forms, but the realistic goals of the antislavery Kentuckians in 1792 was to have the new constitution provide for emancipation in principle and to place some restrictions upon the further importation of slaves. Then perhaps a future legislature at some propitious moment could proceed with a scheme for gradual emancipation.

Father Rice made the case for the antislavery element in a major speech to the committee. The institution was unjust and immoral, he declared, because it violated God's natural law of human freedom. All men were equal under God; one should not be compelled to obey another. Rice charged that slavery was bad policy for the community because it breed idleness in the people and weakened political virtue. The impending separation from Virginia gave Kentuckians an opportunity to shed their guilt. "As a separate State, we are just now come to birth, and it depends upon our free choice, whether we shall be born in this sin, or innocent of it." When property rights were cited in defense of slavery, Rice replied that such laws were invalid because they were contrary to the laws of God. Rice many have weakened his argument by shrugging off as inconsequential the possible effects of slavery restrictions upon the economic and population growth of the new state, the possibility that extensive miscegenation would follow emancipation, and the racial complications that might accompany the presence of a large free black population. Many Kentuckians viewed those aspects of slavery and its future with deep concern. Rice's cause was also harmed by the inability of the antislavery people to agree upon one definite program.[17]

Nicholas was the main defender of slavery in the convention. He cited history and the Bible to prove that slavery had always existed, and he argued that the Tenth Convention could not prohibit slavery because the compact with Virginia had provided for the protection of property rights. Property could not be taken without compensation to the owner, and Nicholas declared that Kentucky could not possibly afford the costs of emancipation. He agreed that individual masters should be allowed to free their own slaves at their own expense, but he denied that it could be done by the state. If the antislavery advocates were really sincere, he jibed, why did so many of them own slaves? Nicholas asserted that non-slaveholders who sought emancipation were motivated by jealousy of slaveholders. If Negroes were equal to whites, he argued, the convention was illegal since Negroes had not been able to vote for delegates. If the slaves had a valid claim to freedom, the Indians owned all the land in the United States. Mass emancipation would result in miscegenation and racial debasement, Nicholas concluded. Slavery was good for the Kentucky economy, and it attracted the ideal type of settler.

The antislavery advocates maintained that the proposed bill of rights applied to slaves when it declared that "all men were created equal." Nicholas moved to block that interpretation by substituting for it the phrase "all men, when they form a social compact, are equal." He also placed in the tentative constitution severe restrictions on the actions that future legislatures could take. Emancipation would be possible only with the consent of the master and payment for the full value of the slave. While the commercial importation of slaves could be halted by the legislature, immigrants could not be prohibited from bringing their slaves into the state.

The climax to the slavery debate came a week later on Wednesday, April 18 when pesky Sam Taylor of Mercer County moved to eliminate Article IX, the slavery section on which the committee had been working. James Smith of Bourbon County seconded his motion. Had it passed, the legislature would have been free to deal with the slavery issue without any constitutional restrictions. However, the motion failed, 16 to 26, in the only recorded vote of the entire convention. All of the 26 members of the majority held slaves, but so did 12 of the 16 who voted in the minority. On the average, the proslavery delegates owned more slaves and more land than did their opponents. Yet personal economics did not explain all of the votes. James Garrard, for example, was a wealthy planter with 23 slaves, but he voted antislavery, apparently from religious convictions. The six ministers who remained after Rice's resignation (John Bailey, George Smith and James Garrard, Baptists; James Crawford and Benedict Swope, Presbyterians; Charles Kavenaugh, Methodist) all voted to discard Article IX. Hubbard Taylor testified to Nicholas' influence when he wrote Madison that he and others would have been glad to halt immediately the importation of slaves for sale and all importation at some specified date in the future, "but Colo. Nicholas wd. not give up the plan adopted in the Resolve for that purpose."[18]

The committee continued its work on Thursday with Shelby in the chair. The results of its labors became apparent the next day. Ignoring any negative implications of Friday, April 13, Garrard reported to the convention a series of 22 resolutions that became the basis for the writing of the constitution. They represented in the main the thinking of George Nicholas, although he was not able to impose his will in all instances. Resolution 12 called for the governor to be elected by an electoral college; Nicholas had wanted direct election by the voters. Some further changes were made in committee, some other modifications occurred on the floor of the convention, but in a large measure the resolutions in their final form reflected his concept of what the new state government could and should be. Nicholas was a political realist who accepted compromise and even defeat when he could not get all that he wanted. "The idea of perfection in government is a mere chimera," he warned. "The most to be hoped for is the greater not the perfect good." And he insisted that "Experience is the best if not the only safe teacher."

Among their major points, the resolutions called for separation of powers, a two house legislature, free white male suffrage without property qualifications, representatives allocated by population, senators elected at large by electors but with each county having as least one, a governor elected for a four year term by electors with no restriction on re-election, public elections by ballot, no legislative power to free slaves without the consent of the owner or without payment of the full value of the slaves, no legislative power to prohibit emigrants from bringing slaves into the state, legislative power to halt the importation of slaves for sale and to provide for humane treatment, sheriffs and coroners to be elected, the Virginia compact to be declared a part of the constitution, the state Supreme Court to have original and final jurisdiction in land cases unless the legislature rescinded the original jurisdiction provision if it did not prove beneficial, another convention to be held in __ years to make needed changes in the constitution if a majority of those voting for representatives in two elections decided that such a convention should be held.[19]

Nicholas then introduced another resolution that may not have been considered in committee and which was not usually included in a constitution. Recognizing that considerable competition might develop over the location of a state capital, he proposed the creation of a five man committee to bargain with interested communities over inducements that might be offered and to make the final selection. The resolution also provided that the site selected could not be changed except with the consent of two-thirds of both houses of the legislature. His resolution received two readings and was accepted by the convention.[20]

Then a select committee of ten was appointed "to prepare a Constitution and make report thereon on Tuesday next. . . ." Nicholas was the obvious choice for chairman. The other members of the drafting committee were: Thomas Lewis, Fayette County; Benjamin Sebastian and Alexander S. Bullitt, Jefferson; James Garrard, Bourbon; Cuthbert Harrison, Nelson; Thomas Kennedy, Madison; Isaac Shelby, Lincoln; Caleb Wallace, Woodford; and Thomas Waring, Mason. Since Nicholas was from Mercer County, all counties were represented with only Jefferson having two members on the committee.[21] Had talent received more attention and geographical location less, the composition of the committee would have been somewhat different. Certainly, Harry Innes and Samuel McDowell could have contributed more than some of the members appointed. But that was of little consequence, for the convention delegates must have realized the George Nicholas would be the primary author of Kentucky's first constitution. With little to do until the drafting committee reported, the convention adjourned until Tuesday, April 17, leaving ten of its members to work over the long weekend.

The Tuesday session opened with Chairman Nicholas presenting the draft of a constitution that was quickly referred to the committee-of-the-whole. Later that day Chairman Garrard reported that the committee had accepted several amendments to the draft constitution. He was prepared to report them, but the convention decided to adjourn until Wednesday morning. Excellent progress had been made, and on Wednesday, when he wrote a Virginia friend, Sam McDowell expressed satisfaction with what had been done. "Our Convention have been sitting two weeks past framing the Constitution for Kentucky and will finish tomorrow. And I think we will have a tolerable good Constitution."[22]

On Wednesday, April 18, Garrard presented the changes made by the committee-of-the-whole, and the convention accepted them. Article I was changed to allow elections to be held over a three day period if the presiding officer or officers considered it necessary. Article I was also amended to allow the legislature to change the date of its annual meeting and to prohibit ministers of "religious societies" from serving in the General Assembly. As a concession to the antislavery element, Article IX was altered to make emancipation somewhat easier. Instead of the legislature having full power to provide for individual emancipation, it was ordered by the constitution to make such provision available.

Nicholas then took the floor and moved several amendments to the schedule that provided for an orderly transition to statehood. One of them provided that crimes allegedly committed under Virginia law prior to June 1, 1792 would be treated as if done in Kentucky after statehood was achieved. Another amendment made the county sheriff or a deputy the election officer but authorized a justice of the peace to serve if the sheriff or deputy refused or neglected to do so. Election officials were also empowered to administer an oath of eligibility to prospective voters, and elections were directed to be held at the places in each county assigned for holding courts. The convention accepted all of these late amendments. After the antislavery people made and lost their motion to strike all of Article IX, the constitution as amended was ordered "to be fairly transcribed," entered in the journal, and read again in convention on Thursday, April 19.[23]

The convention, thanks largely to George Nicholas, had moved with surprising rapidity, and the end was near. The constitution was read again on Thursday morning and "was then agreed to as the constitution for the government of the state of Kentucky." President McDowell was requested to transmit a copy to the president of the United States and to arrange for the preservation of the convention's records until the legislature of the new state directed their future custody. "In Testimony of the authenticity of the foregoing Journals of the Convention," Samuel McDowell signed and sealed the journal and Clerk Thomas Todd attested his signature. No other member signed, and the constitution was not submitted to the voters for their ratification. "The Convention then adjourned."[24]

In addition to the pride they had in the completion of their work, the delegates to the constitution convention received a token compensation for their efforts. The first General Assembly provided payments of $20 to the president, $12 to each member, $50 to the clerk, $12 to the sergeant-at-arms and $10 to the doorkeeper. No payment had been made to members of the earlier conventions.[25]

The long road to statehood was almost at an end. In six weeks, on June 1, 1792, Kentucky would become the fifteenth state in the United States of America. Few if any determined dissenters remained to challenge the decision that had been made, although there was continued opposition to some provisions in the constitution, particularly the protection of slavery and the original jurisdiction of the Supreme Court in land cases. Doubt still lingered in some minds about the ability of Kentuckians to turn the document into a viable government. As word of the work of the Tenth Convention filtered across Kentucky, interested citizens must have wondered: What is in our constitution? Can the government it describes actually work?

SIX

The Constitution Achieved

Kentucky has held four constitutional conventions during the past two hundred years. The first one, in 1792, met for thirteen working sessions within a span of eighteen days and produced a document that occupies just under seventeen pages of type. Each convention since then has met for a longer period and has written a longer constitution than its predecessor. The 1890-1891 convention conducted its deliberations over a period of nearly eight months and produced a constitution some seven times as long as the 1792 model.[1]

George Nicholas and the others who helped write the 1792 constitution did not even consider creating an original form of government. Utopianism was not among their aspirations. They hoped to establish as quickly as possible a government that would be adequate for the needs of the new state and would be acceptable to most of its citizens. Believing that experience was the most reliable guide to what was needed, they looked to profit from the experience of the states already in the Union. Certainly, they hoped to avoid some of the mistakes that had been made elsewhere. The delegates had considerable knowledge about the Virginia government under which they would live until June 1, 1792, but they were as concerned with its weaknesses as with its strengths. The Virginia constitution was not the major source upon which they drew. The ratification debates over the federal constitution were still fresh in mind; some of the convention delegates had probably read *The Federalist Papers,* which had discussed the proposed constitution in great detail. Several members of the Tenth Convention were familiar with the constitutions of other states. James Smith of Bourbon County had served in the 1776 Pennsylvania Convention.

The Pennsylvania constitution of 1776 was one of the most radical adopted during the revolutionary era as the thirteen colonies transformed themselves into states. The state's leaders were preoccupied with the war and the establishment of independence, and the convention was dominated by the element that in Kentucky was called partisans. A conservative postwar reaction led to a thorough revision in 1790 that moderated much of the earlier version. The new constitution was still one of the most democratic in the nation, but few people called it radical. Nicholas and at least some of his colleagues were familiar with the 1790 document and used it extensively in their drafting. They also used the 1776 version for things to be avoided.

John D. Barnhart concluded after a careful study of the origins of the Kentucky constitution of 1792 that seventy-five of its 107 sections "were so similar as to justify the statement that Pennsylvania's constitution was their model." He found a close similarity in twenty-seven of the twenty-eight sections in the Bill of Rights, in fourteen of seventeen sections dealing with the executive branch, and in eighteen of twenty-nine sections describing the legislature and its operation. He classified twenty sections as being original with the Tenth Convention, most of them concentrated in Articles IX, X, and XI. Five sections were derived from the Maryland constitution, three from the constitution of the United States, and one from the South Carolina constitution.[2] (For the text of the 1792 Kentucky Constitution, see pages 152-68.)

No member of the 1792 convention believed that they had written a perfect constitution. Despite his great influence, George Nicholas was defeated on several important issues, and the final product contained a number of pragmatic compromises between what was ideal and what was realistic. Perhaps the best indication of how the founders viewed their handiwork was the unusual provision in Article XI for the possible holding of another convention as early as 1799.[3] This invitation to revise in the near future indicated clearly that the Tenth Convention did not consider its product to be sacrosanct.

The constitution created some confusion over the name of the political entity for which it outlined a frame of government. The brief preamble referred to the people of "the State of Kentucky," but the last section of the "Schedule" declared that "The Government of the Commonwealth of Kentucky shall commence on the first day of June next." Most of the references in the document were to "Commonwealth," and that must have been the name the drafters intended should be used.

The framers of the state constitutions during the early years of independence were determined to avoid establishing a possible tyranny; a small number of persons must not be allowed to control the government. The Kentucky constitution makers of 1792 followed this principle. In their bill of rights they asserted that men "have at all times an unalienable and indefeasible right to alter, reform, or abolish their government," based on the inherent power of the people. But they sought methods to make the government safe without having to resort to drastic change. Article I ordered that "the powers of government shall be divided into three distinct departments, each of them confided to a separate body of magistracy," and that "no person, or collection of persons, being of one of these departments, shall exercise any power properly belonging to either of the others, except in the instances hereinafter expressly permitted." But absolute separation in itself presented a possible danger; left unhampered, a portion the government might grow like a political cancer until it dominated the other two branches. Therefore, the framers included in the document a system of checks and balances that violated the principle of absolute separation of powers. It made for a safer if less efficient political system.

During the late colonial period the legislatures often represented the wishes of the discontented people while the governors often symbolized hated authority. In keeping with this experience, the Kentucky constitution devoted considerably more attention to the legislature (Article I) than to either the executive or the judicial branch. The General Assembly that emerged from their deliberations was a bicameral body that represented a compromise between radical and conservative desires. The most radical partisans had sought a one-house body with annual elections based on universal white manhood suffrage. Conservatives were more likely to favor property requirements for voting and a bicameral legislature with higher qualifications and longer terms for members of the upper house than for those of the lower chamber. The constitution called for representatives to be elected annually, with the number based upon the free adult male population instead of county representation, as used in Virginia. To provide a count of the free adult male population, a state census would be conducted each four years; the ten-year federal interval was too long. A special power of the lower house was its monopoly over the origination of money bills.[4]

In contrast to the democratic House elections, the senators were to be chosen by electors who were elected by the voters each four years. These electors would then assemble in May to elect for four-year terms senators who were "men of the most wisdom, experience, and virtue." Each county would have a senator; others could be elected at large from anywhere in the state.[5]

The age requirements for legislators were somewhat lower than they were for members of the federal Congress. In part, that may have reflected the belief that state legislators would not be confronted by as serious and complex issues as would those in Congress. In part, the lower requirements may have reflected conditions in a frontier state where immigration was still heavy, many citizens had short residence in the commonwealth, and the age of citizens was under the average of the seaboard states.

Both the electors and the legislators were to receive six shillings a day for active service, including travel time. That sum could be changed by the General Assembly, but the change could not take effect during the existence of the legislature that made the change. No member of the General Assembly during the term for which he was elected or for one year thereafter could "be appointed to any civil office under this State, which shall have been created, or the emoluments of which shall have been increased, during the time such Senator or Representative was in office." Members of the first legislature were exempted from that provision; they might be needed to staff positions in the new government, and they would probably create a number of posts during their term.

As one of the usual requirements and procedures, each house was authorized to expel a member by a two-thirds vote. But the voters were the expelled member's court of last resort. Since a member could not be twice expelled for the same reason, he could in effect appeal to his constituents and receive vindication and political absolution through reelection.

Some members of the Tenth Convention wanted to exclude lawyers from the legislature. They were not able to do so, but ministers of religious societies, members of Congress, and anyone holding an "office of profit" under either the United States or Kentucky was excluded from the General Assembly. The only exceptions were attorneys, justices of the peace, militia officers, and coroners during the periods when they acted in such capacities. Each legislator (and each sheriff) was required to swear (or affirm) that he had not given or promised any bribe or treat to secure his election.[6]

Nicholas had to strike a delicate balance in defining the powers of the legislature. The fear of executive tyranny was still so strong that the General Assembly had to be a powerful body, and he had to heed the demand for a democratic system of representation. But he wanted to avoid having a legislature that could dominate the rest of the government, and he feared that a too radical lower house might threaten property rights, especially those of large landholders. Many Kentuckians would be delighted if large plantations were broken up. A strong executive could check the legislature if it strayed too far from its proper functions, and the House would be checked by a Senate composed of the most able men in the state, who were elected indirectly for four-year terms. Furthermore, if the senators were elected at large from the entire state, they would avoid the dangers of excessive localism. Nicholas got much of what he wanted, although he had to accept the assignment of at least one senator to a county.[7]

The early state constitutions had usually provided for a weak executive, elected for a brief term and denied many of the powers and functions of the late colonial governors. The 1792 constitution reversed that trend. Kentucky's chief executive was probably more powerful than any other governor of that era. Article II gave him the veto power over legislation, he had extensive appointive powers, his four-year term was the longest for any governor at that time, and he could succeed himself. The succession provision was based at least in part upon the fear that Kentucky had so few people well qualified for office that a short, single term might quickly deplete the pool of qualified personnel.

The Tenth Convention rejected Nicholas's recommendation that the governor be elected by direct popular vote. Instead, it decided upon an electoral system. The governor, who must be thirty years old and a state resident for two years before his election, was to be chosen by the electors for the Senate at the same time and place and in the same manner as the senators were elected. The constitution did not provided for a lieutenant-governor. If a vacancy occurred, the Speaker of the Senate would "exercise the office of Governor until another shall be duly qualified." The chief executive was commander-in-chief of the state's army, navy, and militia except when the latter was called into federal service. He could appoint, "with the advice and consent of the Senate," the state officials whose appointments were not otherwise provided for. The major exceptions were the sheriffs and coroners, who were elected for three-year terms, the militia company officers, who were elected by their men, the court clerks, who were appointed by the court each served, and the state treasurer, who was elected annually by a joint vote of the General Assembly.

The Kentucky governor's chief assistants were the attorney general and the secretary of state, both of whom he appointed. The attorney general was to represent the Commonwealth in all criminal cases and in the superior courts in civil cases. It was not a full-time position, and the holder of the position could continue his own legal practice. The governor and both houses of the General Assembly could ask for his legal opinion on issues. The secretary of state, appointed for the duration of the governor's term, "if he shall so long behave himself well," was the custodian of the register in which he was to record all official acts and proceedings of the executive office. Upon request, he was required to submit all such records to either house of the General Assembly.[8] This was another check upon executive power; a governor could not conceal his actions behind a veil of secrecy.

The governor's other listed powers were extensive.[9] Since the formation of state governments during the Revolution, most governors had been much weaker than the legislatures; the Tenth Convention aimed to redress that balance in Kentucky.

The brief Article III contained one of the most democratic provisions of the new constitution, one that was considered radical by many people of that era. The right to vote was extended to free male citizens twenty-one years of age who had lived in the state for two years or in the county where they voted for one year. No property or religious qualification was required. Only four years earlier in Virginia, George Nicholas had advocated tax payment or militia service as a suffrage requirement, but in 1792 he wrote that "the most serious reflection has convinced me that such qualifications are inadmissible in a free state." In abandoning his earlier stance, Nicholas argued that a large electorate would add stability to the government by involving more people in its processes and would reduce bribery and other corrupt election practices by making them too expensive for most politicians. He also contended that the assurance of liberal political rights would attract more immigrants to the state. Conservatives should not be alarmed, Nicholas confided to Madison, for in nineteen cases out of twenty, a wealthy candidate would be elected over a poor one. "The Senate," he predicted, "will be composed altogether of men of that class. I will give up my opinion as soon as I see a man in rags chosen to that body." Even the House of Representatives "will therefore always have a majority at least of its members men of property." Kentucky did have some free black males who were not specifically excluded from voting; Article III did not list "white" as a requirement. But blacks were not considered to be citizens, and the use of that term disqualified them from voting. The constitution required the use of ballots in elections instead of voice voting, a change that was also considered a democratic reform that would reduce the possibility of powerful individuals controlling elections. But, as spelled out in the 1792 election law, the ballot was not truly secret. Each voter was to hand his unfolded ballot to the sheriff, who might easily glimpse the vote. Even after the law was amended to require that the ballot be folded, an inquisitive sheriff might ascertain the preference while making sure that only one ballot had been presented.[10]

Kentucky's constitution makers recognized that upon occasion the governor and other civil officers might need to be removed from office. Following the federal process, Article IV made all civil officials liable for impeachment by the House of Representatives for misdemeanors committed while in office. Trial would be by the Senate, with a two-thirds vote of those present required to convict. The judgment could not go beyond removal from office and disqualification from holding any state office of honor, trust, or profit in the future, but the convicted party was also subject to indictment, trial, and possible punishment under the laws of the state.[11]

For establishing a court system the Kentucky constitution, like the federal one, left the legislature broad discretion in creating the inferior courts. It decreed that there should be one supreme court known as the Court of Appeals and "such inferior courts as the Legislature may, from time to time, ordain and establish." Since the courts were inherently weaker than the other two branches of government, the judges' independence was protected by appointments "during good behavior," and "adequate compensation," which could not be diminished during a judge's continuance in office. But for reasonable cause that fell short of grounds for impeachment, the governor could remove a judge upon address by two-thirds of both houses of the legislature. The governor was directed to appoint a "competent number" of justices of the peace for indefinite terms in each county. They too could be removed for cause upon the address of two-thirds of each house of the General Assembly.[12]

The Court of Appeals, as the name indicates, had appellate jurisdiction in most cases, but Nicholas insisted that it must also have original jurisdiction in land cases. This provision became one of the most controversial features of the new constitution. Some people suspected Nicholas of sponsoring the unusual provision for selfish reasons. As Kentucky's most noted attorney, he could expect lucrative fees for appearances before the commonwealth's highest court. While he was undoubtedly aware of the advantages that could accrue to him, his main concern was to untangle the mass of land suits that clogged the District's courts and left titles in doubt for many years. He would expedite settlements by giving the Court of Appeals original jurisdiction in such cases and directing it "to do right and justice to the parties, with as little delay and at as small an expense as the nature of the business will allow." A jury would be used to determine facts not agreed upon by the parties involved unless they waived their rights to trial by jury. Each judge was to render his opinion in open court, and dissenters were to present their opposing opinions in writing for the court record. Nicholas encountered considerable opposition, but he won his way after agreeing to insert a specific provision that the legislature could change the procedure or "take away entirely the original jurisdiction hereby given to the said court in such cases."[13]

Article VI dealt largely with minor officers, although in an era of restricted travel they acquired extensive powers. As a concession to local democracy, and in a sharp departure from Virginia's practice, sheriffs and coroners were to be elected in each county for three-year terms; the sheriff could not be elected or appointed twice in a six-year period. The "free men of this Commonwealth" were to be "armed and disciplined for its defense," but conscientious objectors were allowed to avoid militia duty by paying an equivalent for personal service in lieu of it. The governor was to appoint militia officers above the company level except for the battalion staff officers, whose appointments would be made by the unit's field officers. Each court was authorized to appoint a clerk, whose tenure was during good behavior. A candidate for court clerk had to possess a certificate of qualifications from the Court of Appeals.[14]

Members of the General Assembly and all executive and judicial officers were required to take a prescribed oath (or to affirm) before assuming office: "I do solemnly swear (or affirm, as the case may be), that I will be faithful and true to the Commonwealth of Kentucky, so long as I continue a citizen thereof, and that I will faithfully execute, to the best of my abilities, the office of ——, according to law." The method of administering the oath was to "be such as is most consistent with the conscience of the deponent, and shall be esteemed by the Legislature the most solemn appeal to God."[15] (The dueling anachronism that has attracted derision as the Commonwealth nears the twenty-first century was not added until the 1850 constitution.)

Several unrelated subjects that had to be included somewhere were grouped in Article VIII. The definition of treason was taken directly from the federal constitution, including the provision that conviction had to come from confession in open court or from the testimony of two witnesses to the overt act. Laws were ordered made to exclude from office and the suffrage persons convicted of high crimes and misdemeanors and to prohibit "improper practices" in regard to elections. No money could be drawn from the treasury except by appropriation, army appropriations could not be for longer than one year, and an accounting of public revenues and expenditures was to be made annually. The General Assembly was told to decide what suits could be brought against the Commonwealth and in which courts they could be tried. Virginia laws consistent with the Kentucky constitution and general in nature would remain in force in Kentucky until altered or repealed by the legislature. And the compact with Virginia, including any changes that might be made, was to be considered as if it were a part of the constitution.[16]

Writing soon after the Tenth Convention adjourned, George Nicholas admitted that "the clause respecting slaves will I expect bring on us the severe animadversions of our N[orthern] brethren." Article IX would probably not have been included in the constitution, he added, "if the friends to emancipation had not been so clamorous on that subject, as well in the convention as out of it, so to make it necessary either to give up that property or to secure it." Virginia law considered slaves to be property, he added; if they were freed their owners would have to be compensated, but Kentucky could not possibly bear that expense. The Kentucky endorsement of slavery did not add a single slave to the number in the country; the only difference would be the location of some slaves within the country. Furthermore, Nicholas asserted, prohibition of slavery would discourage "valuable immigrants" from coming to live in the state.[17]

Article IX provided the constitutional sanction for slavery. The legislature was forbidden to provide for emancipation without the consent of the owner or without providing full compensation for the slaves freed. Immigrants could not be prohibited from bringing in their slaves, but the legislature could prevent the entry of slaves as merchandise or those brought in from a foreign country, including those imported into the United States after January 1, 1789. The legislature was directed to pass laws that would allow masters to free their own slaves, provided the freedmen did not become a public charge to the county. The legislature was also given full power to require humane treatment or to have ill-treated slaves sold for their protection, but to the master's benefit.[18] The future would show the near impossibility of convicting a master of ill treatment when the testimony of slaves was not allowed.

Article X consisted of a detailed method for selecting the "Seat of Government," a subject not usually found in constitutions. Disagreements over location were inevitable, and this provision at least provided an orderly method for reaching a decision. In its 1792 session the House of Representatives was directed to select twenty-one persons by ballot. Then the mem-

bers from Fayette and Mercer counties would alternately eliminate names until only five remained. As a location committee,
these five men would select a site, lay off a town, receive gifts
and grants, and negotiate with the owners of the land selected.
The General Assembly and the Court of Appeals were to hold
their sessions there in not more than five years. Moving from
the site chosen would require a two-thirds vote of both houses
of the legislature.[19]

Nicholas was by no means the only person who believed
that another constitutional convention should be held within a
few years. That had been one of James Madison's suggestions,
and there was no serious objection to the proposal in the Tenth
Convention. Nicholas originally thought of waiting only three
or four years, but the convention decided on seven. By then,
Nicholas hoped, the state would have more talented citizens
who could be coopted into the political process, and experience would have indicated where improvements should be
made. He did not propose that the state have periodic reviews
of its constitution at frequent intervals. The initial government
was temporary in nature; once its weaknesses had been cor-
rected, future changes should be rare.

The scheme outlined in Article XI depended upon voter
approval. If a majority of those voting for representatives in
1797 and 1798 favored a constitutional convention, the General Assembly at its next session would provide for its calling "for
the purpose of readopting, amending or changing this Constitution." If the voters rejected the proposed convention, one
could be called at any time by a two-thirds vote of both houses
of the legislature.[20] The 1792 constitution made no provision
for adding amendments on an individual basis, and popular
ratification was not required for any changes that might be
made. This invitation to review and change showed that the
delegates to the Tenth Convention did not consider their handiwork inviolable. They did the best they could under the conditions of their day, but they realized that experience with the
new government might well indicate the need for improvement.

Before the Tenth Convention met, ten amendments had

been added to the federal constitution as a Bill of Rights. That example may have helped determine the location of the twenty-eight sections that made up the Kentucky Bill of Rights. Instead of preceding the constitution, Article XII was the last of the regular articles. The danger of appearing to declare that slaves had equal rights with whites was avoided by stating in Section 1 that "all men, when they form a social compact, are equal." Since slaves (and free blacks) had not been involved in the formation of the constitution, they were not equal and were not entitled to the protection of the Bill of Rights. In future years Section 2 would be cited often in defense of state's rights, including the formation in 1861 of a Confederate state of Kentucky. It asserted that "all power is inherent in the people, and all free governments are founded on their authority, and instituted for their peace, safety and happiness. For the advancement of these ends, they have at all times an unalienable and indefeasible right to alter, reform, or abolish their government, in such manner as they may think proper." Article XII continued with statements on religious freedom, free elections, equal justice, freedom of expression, unreasonable searches and seizures, peaceable assembly, bills of attainder, and similar topics that had become almost standard in constitutions in the United States. The last section, number 28, was designed to solidify the other clauses: "*We Declare,* that every-thing in this article is excepted out of the general powers of government, and shall forever remain inviolate; and that all laws contrary thereto or contrary to this Constitution shall be void."[21]

A "Schedule" of eleven sections, added after Article XII, was designed to speed and ease the formation of the new government with minimal disruption. Existing legal arrangements such as contracts, claims, and prosecutions were to be as valid as if the new government had not been formed. Civil and military officers commissioned by Virginia would continue to hold office until August 10, 1792. (Many of them were then reappointed to the same positions but under authority of the Commonwealth of Kentucky.) Until the census required in Article I was made, county representation in the House was set at: Fayette, 9; Nelson, 6; Bourbon, 5; Lincoln, Mercer, and Woodford, 4 each; Madison and Jefferson, 3; and Mason, 2. The General Assembly was to meet in Lexington on June 4, less than seven weeks from the close of the Tenth Convention. The governor was authorized to use his own seal until the state procured one. Until the legislature decided otherwise, oaths of office could be administered by a justice of the peace. Offenses under Virginia law committed within the District of Kentucky prior to June 1, 1792, were to be considered as if committed against the Commonwealth of Kentucky after that date. Election rules were spelled out in some detail. And, finally, "The Government of the Commonwealth of Kentucky shall commence on the first day of June next."[22]

This constitution was relatively brief and was written in some haste, but it succeeded in dealing with most of the topics one would expect to find in such a document. The glaring absence was public education. Nowhere did the 1792 constitution mention the need for a system of public schools. The omission is inexplicable in view of the emphasis placed upon the broad expansion of suffrage to include all free, white, adult males. Historically, an expansion of the suffrage has been accompanied by—or even preceded by—a demand for at least rudimentary schooling to prepare better qualified citizen voters. Private schools had existed in Kentucky from the early days of settlement. Mrs. William Comes's dame school at Fort Harrod in 1775 was probably the first, but it was soon followed by several others. Payment was a problem for many parents, and few of the early schools survived for long. In 1780 the Virginia legislature granted 8,000 acres for the support of a public school or seminary in Kentucky. Transylvania Seminary was established three years later, although a teacher was not employed until 1785.[23] Private schools were not providing an adequate system of education.

At least one of the numerous correspondents of the *Kentucky Gazette* advocated the creation of public schools during the pre-convention discussions in the newspaper's columns. "Philanthropus" outlined a system, much like a Thomas Jefferson proposal, that would have provided a minimum education for the mass of the people and produced leaders for the state. He wanted his plan incorporated in the constitution so that future legislatures would not be able to curtail or abolish it. In his scheme counties would be divided into "hundreds," each four or five miles square, which would bear the expense of three-year public schools that would concentrate on reading, writing, and arithmetic. Each year a supervisor would select the boy of "best genius" whose parents could not afford additional schooling for him. The chosen lads would be sent at public expense to one of the seven or eight grammar schools that would be established in various parts of the state. There they would study Greek, Latin, geography, and higher mathematics for one or two years. Each year seven or eight "geniuses" would be picked from these schools to continue their education at public expense. About half of them would have their education terminated after six years; many of them would then teach in the grammar schools. The top half would go on to a state university. From this select group would come many of the leaders of the state.[24]

Philanthropus's plea and plan went unheeded, and available records do not indicate that public education was even discussed at the constitutional convention. That initial neglect reflects an attitude toward education that, with a few occasional exceptions, has plagued Kentucky and retarded its economic and social progress for nearly two centuries. As historian Thomas D. Clark has written, "Whatever else pioneering emigrants lugged across the Appalachians in the late eighteenth century, they seem not to have brought along a burning zeal to educate their children."[25]

The *Kentucky Gazette* began publishing extracts from the new constitution on April 28; complete copies were on sale in Mr. Bradford's office by May 12. Most of the Kentuckians who read the document were reasonably well pleased with it, although few would have given it unqualified praise. Much of the lingering criticisms centered around the original jurisdiction of the Court of Appeals in land cases, the protection given slavery, and such "autocratic" features as the electoral college that seemed designed to curb majority rule. The constitution represented an adroit blend of features that had some appeal to most citizens. Radicals were pleased by the elimination of religious and property qualifications for voting, by the use of ballots in elections, by the annual elections for representatives and the popular election of many local officers, and by the quadrennial reapportionment of the lower house. Conservatives who might have balked at such democratic excesses were reassured by the two-house legislature, the electoral college, the creation of a strong executive, the careful separation of powers, and the detailed bill of rights.

The Kentucky constitution was one of the most liberal state constitutions in the country, but it was not a radical document. It reassured some seaboard conservatives who had feared that it would reflect excesses of frontier democracy. Much to their relief, the constitution of the first transmontane state suggested that the new states in the West might retain much of their eastern heritage. It was a constitution that most of the country could accept without serious concern. It was a constitution that most Kentuckians could live with and under.

The constitution's primary author reported the results of the convention to James Madison in a letter of May 2, 1792: "We have formed our government which I believe you will think is not the worst in the Union."[26] The next task was to put the government into operation as soon as possible. The road to statehood had seemed endless at times to some of the people who had traveled it, but Kentucky was still very young. No adult Kentuckian in 1792 had been born in Kentucky.

SEVEN

Implementing the Constitution

The 1792 elections in Kentucky may have been the most non-partisan in the long and usually controversial political history of the commonwealth. In the absence of organized political parties to select candidates and draft platforms, and with most candidates unwilling to appear to seek office, Kentuckians saw little overt campaigning. Some voters must have exchanged opinions and espoused the selection of favored individuals, but in the main they simply voted for the men whom they believed were best qualified to hold positions in the new government. In doing so, they came close to meeting the ideal for holding elections in that era.

Little time remained between the adjournment of the Tenth Convention on April 19 and June 1, when Kentucky was to become a state. The *Kentucky Gazette* of April 21, 1792, contained a call for the election of representatives, electors, sheriffs and coroners at the county courthouses on Tuesday, May 1. The announcement listed the qualifications for each office as well as for the voters; the oaths for sheriffs and prospective voters were also included. These elections took place as scheduled, apparently without significant incident, and the newspaper published the results, as follows, without indicating the votes cast.[1]

Representatives	Electors

Fayette County

Representatives	Electors
William Russell	William Campbell
John Hawkins	Edward Payne
Thomas Lewis	John Martin
Hubbard Taylor	Abraham Bowman
James Trotter	Robert Todd
Joseph Crockett	John Bradford
James McMillin	John Morrison
John McDowell	Gabriel Madison
Robert Patterson	Peyton Short
Sheriff: Thomas Clarke	Coroner: John Maxwell

Lincoln County

Representatives	Electors
William Montgomery	John Logan
Henry Pawling	Benjamin Logan
James Davis	Isaac Shelby
Jeff Cravens	Thomas Todd
Sheriff: William Montgomery	Coroner: Richard Jachman

Mercer County

Representatives	Electors
Samuel Taylor	Christopher Greenup
John Jouett	Harry Innes
Jacob Frowman	Samuel McDowell
Robert Mosby	William Kennedy
Sheriff: Benjamin Letcher	Coroner: Walter E. Strong

Madison County

Representatives	Electors
Higgarson Grubbs	William Irvin
Thomas Clay	Higgarson Grubbs
John Miller	Thomas Clay
Sheriff: Thomas Gass	Coroner: Christopher Harris, Jr.

Bourbon County

Representatives	Electors
George M. Bedinger	John Edwards
John Waller	Benjamin Harrison

Charles Smith   Thomas Jones
James Smith   Andrew Hood
John McKenny   John Allen
Sheriff: John Gregg   Coroner: Thomas Hallock

Woodford County

John Watkins   John Watkins
Richard Young   George Muter
William Steele   Richard Young
John Grant   Robert Johnson
Sheriff: John Craig   Coroner: William Cave

Jefferson County

Richard Taylor   Alexander S. Bullitt
Robert Breckenridge [*sic*]   Richard C. Anderson
Benjamin Roberts   John Campbell
Sheriff: William Sullivan   Coroner: Richard Eastin

Nelson County

William King   Walter Beall
Robert Able   John Caldwell
Matthew Walton   William May
Edmund Thomas   Cuthbert Harrison
Joseph Hobbs   Adam Shepherd
Joshua Hobbs   James Chambers
Sheriff: Benjamin Pope   Coroner: Henry Clift

Mason County

Alexander D. Orr   Robert Rankin
John Wilson   George Stockton
Sheriff: Miles W. Conway   Coroner: David Brodrick

Two weeks later, on May 15, the electors met in Lexington and elected Isaac Shelby as Kentucky's first governor. The vote was not given in the brief newspaper announcement, but on June 8 in its reply to the governor's message the House of Representatives called it "almost unanimous." The electors also performed their dual function of electing the eleven senators who made up the upper house of the first General Assembly. Nine were elected by county; the other two were elected from the state at large. The county senators were: John Campbell, Jefferson; John Logan, Lincoln; Richard Todd, Fayette; John Caldwell, Nelson; William McDowell, Mercer; Thomas Kennedy, Madison; John Allen, Bourbon; Robert Johnson, Woodford; and Alexander D. Orr, Mason. Alexander S. Bullitt, Jefferson, and Peyton Short, Fayette, were elected at large.[2] Aspirants for Senate membership who were members of the electoral college had a decided advantage over nonmembers. Eight of the eleven senators had been electors, as had Isaac Shelby, the newly elected governor.

Shelby was born near Hagerstown, Maryland, on December 11, 1750, to General Evan and Letitia Cox Shelby. Little is known of his boyhood except that he received scant formal education. The family moved to the West in 1772 and built a store and fort near present-day Bristol on the Virginia-North Carolina line. Lieutenant Shelby served in his father's regiment during Lord Dunmore's War, and he attracted favorable attention for his leadership at the Battle of Point Pleasant in October 1774. Shelby spent parts of several years in the Kentucky area, during which he did some surveying for the Henderson company and claimed good lands for himself. In 1777 he was a commissary of supply for the American army and some frontier posts, and he assisted in negotiations with the Cherokees in an effort to keep them from helping the British. Shelby was elected to the Virginia legislature in 1779 but was not seated when it was discovered that he actually resided in North Carolina. Appointed a colonel in the North Carolina militia, he was locating and surveying Kentucky lands in 1780 when he learned that the British had captured Charleston and the major American army in the South. Shelby returned home, determined to fight until independence was won. He saw active service in several backcountry campaigns and skirmishes, but much of his reputation was earned from his participation in the Battle of King's Mountain on October 7, 1781. This engagement was recognized as one of the turning points in the

Isaac Shelby (1750-1826), Kentucky's first governor (1792-1796), came out of retirement to serve again during the War of 1812 (1812-1816). *Courtesy of The Filson Club, Louisville.*

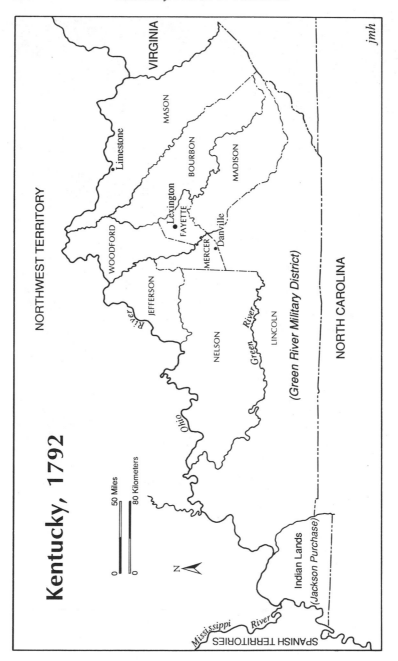

Kentucky, 1792

war in the South, and Shelby's leadership enhanced his reputation.

As the war neared its official end, Shelby moved to his land
in Lincoln County in late 1782. He and his bride, Susannah
Hart Shelby, built an imposing stone house called "Traveler's
Rest" and became famous for their gracious hospitality.
Shelby settled down to the development of his fertile acres. He
had little personal interest in politics, but his wartime experience and a growing reputation for sound, mature judgment led
to his service in several of the conventions, including the constitutional convention of 1792. His frequent selection to chair
the committee-of-the-whole indicated the esteem in which he
was held.

Shelby must have known that he would be a strong candidate for the governorship, but there is no indication that he
sought the position. When he wrote his autobiography years
later, Shelby recalled that when he was elected "he hesitated
some days while the board of electors were sitting to obtain his
own consent to accept an office of such high responsibilities,
and one which he conceived his walk through life had not
qualified him to fill with real advantage to his country or to
himself." His sense of duty and the rapidly nearing date for
statehood must have helped compel his acceptance.[3] The continuing Indian problems—persistent small raids within Kentucky and unsuccessful campaigns north of the Ohio—may
have been a deciding factor. Indian relations was one area in
which he felt competent. Shelby had been active in the militia,
and when elected governor he was serving as sheriff of Lincoln
County.

The governor-elect rode from Traveler's Rest into Danville
on the morning of June 3 on his way to Lexington for his
inauguration on June 4. Christopher Greenup, Thomas Barbee,
and Greenbury Dorsey presented a mercifully brief congrat-
ulatory address on behalf of the citizens of Danville, pledging
"to assist you in the execution of the great trust committed to
your charge." Shelby responded with a carefully worded statement in which he paid respect to "the people of that area
because of his long residence in the neighborhood." He hoped,

"with the assistance of the divine ruler of the Universe, to discharge the trust reposed in me, in such manner as may give general satisfaction to the good people of our infant state."

When Shelby rode out of Danville he was escorted by a detachment of the elite Lexington Troop of Horse. As they neared Lexington he and his escort were joined by the county lieutenant, another troop of horsemen, and the town's trustees, led by chairman John Bradford. When the growing procession reached Main and Cross streets the Light Infantry Company saluted Shelby with military honors and escorted him to his quarters in the Sheaf of Wheat Inn. Then the military units paraded their skills on the public square, fired a salute of fifteen rounds, and concluded the ceremonies with an exuberant discharge of all weapons. Bradford presented Lexington's formal congratulations and welcome, and Shelby responded by confessing his "want of experience and abilities." But he hoped "that, by a strict attention to the duties of my office, and a firm adherence to public justice (both of which I trust are in my power) I may in some degree merit a part of that confidence which they have placed in me." Sometime during that noisy, exciting day, Isaac Shelby was administered the required oath of office by Justice of the Peace Thomas Lewis.[4] Kentucky had a chief executive.

The state, already in its fourth day, also had a legislature. The "Schedule" in the constitution had called for the General Assembly to meet in Lexington on Monday, June 4. The town provided a meeting place, a two-story log structure on Main Street between Broadway and Mill Street. Constructed as a marketplace, it measured twenty-five by fifty feet with the second floor supported on brick pillars. Two days later the legislators thanked the town for "such ample and elegant accommodations." Both houses devoted much of the first two days to organization. The Senate elected Alexander S. Bullitt as its speaker, then employed Buckner Thruston as clerk, Kenneth McKay as sergeant-at-arms, David Johnson as doorkeeper, and the beloved Baptist minister John Gano as chaplain. Robert Breckinridge was elected speaker of the House of Representatives; he and Bullitt were both from Jefferson

County. Thomas Todd was appointed clerk of the House, Nicholas Lewis sergeant-at-arms, Roger Devine doorkeeper, and John Gano was shared with the Senate as chaplain for the General Assembly. Both houses created standing committees and provided some clerical help to assist them in their work. Rules were adopted, much like the ones that had been used in the conventions and much like those of the Virginia legislature. On Tuesday, June 5, each house appointed a committee to confer with its counterpart on how best to receive messages from the governor.[5]

The next day, the dual committees having done their work, the General Assembly notified the governor that the houses were prepared to assemble in the Senate chamber to receive any communication that he might care to deliver. Shelby was prepared for the invitation, and he had decided to deliver his remarks in person. When he and Secretary of State designate James Brown appeared at the doorway at the appointed time, Senate Speaker Bullitt escorted them to the front of the room. Shelby was formally presented to the legislature, then he stood with a short manuscript in hand to deliver his first message to the General Assembly. Many of the members may have wondered how Shelby would perform in his new role, but there could have been few members in the hall who were not acquainted with him.

The legislators saw a solidly built man of forty-one years who had crowded many experiences into his life. Of medium height and powerful body, Shelby had strong features suffused with red. Despite a limited education, he wrote well, but he was not noted for oratory. Shelby did not like to be hurried in making a decision, and he was sometimes criticized for being too slow in making up his mind. But men who knew him well had come to trust his mature judgment; his decisions were usually worth waiting for. While he was willing to accept the responsibility for his gubernatorial acts, he had no desire to force his will upon the legislature; he saw those branches of the government working in harmony to get the government under way. His aversion to officeholding may have dampened any fears of a too-powerful executive. In its reply to his address the

Senate commented: "When we reflect on your well known fondness for privacy and retirement, we cannot sufficiently express our high sense of the obligation which you have conferred on the public."

Shelby's message took only a few minutes. After urging the legislature to adopt measures that would promote "the prosperity of our common country," he made ten suggestions without presenting detailed proposals. In that era a governor would have aroused strong resentment by presenting the draft of a bill for introduction. Legislators were almost uniformly jealous of their prerogatives, so Shelby confined himself largely to the following generalities. The legislature must: 1. Establish public and private credit firmly by "a scrupulous adherence to all public engagements" and "a speedy administration of justice." 2. Give full operation to the constitutional mode for the quick settlement of land disputes. 3. Provide regulations for future elections of the members of the legislature. 4. Keep elections free of undue influence. 5. Appoint two United States senators. 6. Provide for the election of members to the federal House of Representatives. 7. Require sheriffs and other public officials to give security for the proper performance of their duties. 8. Pass laws to compel the proper and humane treatment of slaves. 9. The House must decide how the public revenue was to be raised. "Small as our money resources are," the governor added, "I flatter myself you will find them fully equal to the necessary expenditures of the government." 10. Commissioners must be selected to locate the permanent seat of government.

Shelby assured his listeners of his "hearty co-operation in all your measures which may have a tendency to promote the public good." He concluded by stressing the need for haste because of "the unorganized state of our government and the season of the year." Then he delivered a copy of his remarks to each speaker and withdrew from the chamber.[6]

During the session of twenty-three working days, Governor Shelby worked diligently to solve several urgent problems. He read bills promptly and either signed them or, in one case, returned the measure with his objections in time for amendments to be made. Much of his time was devoted to making appointments to various offices. The most important of these were George Nicholas as attorney-general; Benjamin Logan as major general of militia for the region south of the Kentucky River; Charles Scott as major general of militia north of the Kentucky River; John Hardin, Thomas Kennedy, Robert Todd, and Benjamin Harrison as brigadier-generals for the four brigades into which the militia was divided; William McDowell as state auditor; Harry Innes, Benjamin Sebastian, and Caleb Wallace as justices of the Court of Appeals; George Muter, Samuel McDowell, and Christopher Greenup as justices of the Court of Oyer and Terminer. In addition, as the legislature progressed with its work, Shelby made dozens of appointments for other offices, such as justices of the peace and county surveyors. He also nominated sheriffs for the new counties created during the session, the positions to be held until elections occurred. And he nominated William Montgomery, Sr., for sheriff of Lincoln County in place of one Isaac Shelby, resigned. The Senate accepted all of the governor's nominations.[7] A number of Kentuckians had enough faith in the new government to seek posts of profit in it, and much of Shelby's correspondence consisted of applications from would-be office holders.

The incomplete records of the first state administration do not indicate a great deal about the working relationship between the governor and the General Assembly. They had frequent contacts of a routine nature, such as those involved in transmitting bills and resolutions. The secretary of state was normally the executive courier, while a member of the committee that had drafted a bill usually carried it to the executive branch. Active participation by the governor in the legislative process would not have been considered appropriate, and Shelby made no apparent effort to overstep the bounds of propriety regarding separation of powers. But most of the legislation passed by the General Assembly in its first session was acceptable to the governor, and the Senate's approval of all of his appointments indicated the presence of a harmonious atmosphere. Shelby objected to only one bill during the session. On June 28, as the session neared its close, he returned the measure to create the system of lower courts because of two specific objections. The House quickly amended the bill, the Senate accepted the changes, and the governor signed it.[8]

A historian who studied the first Kentucky legislature commented that "No member rose supremely above the rest for natural or acquired gifts, but, taken as a whole, our first legislature was worthy to be remembered for its ability, its integrity, and its patriotism."[9] While the first General Assembly had no outstanding legislator who dominated its proceedings, it did a workmanlike job in providing the measures essential to the operations of the new government. Its task was eased by the decision to continue Virginia laws in force until they were repealed or amended. Several matters did require immediate attention, but much of the government could continue to operate under existing conditions. Still, the enactment of thirty-seven acts and the adoption of several joint resolutions during a session of only twenty-three working days was a notable legislative achievement.

The two houses moved promptly as the session opened to establish procedures, adopt rules, set up internal organization, and develop working relationships with each other and with the executive branch. The houses usually met at ten o'clock, halted work for a midday dinner, then reassembled at three or four o'clock to continue work into the early evening. The midday interruption was somewhat hazardous; twice the Senate was unable to form a quorum once its members escaped the tedium of legislative procedure. Both houses followed the same general procedure. The introduction of a bill required a day's notice. The introducer of a proposal usually chaired a select committee appointed "to prepare and bring in the same." Most of the work of each house was done in committee-of-the-whole, although amendments were offered and occasionally accepted on the floor of the House or Senate. When the houses disagreed, conference committees were appointed to find a solution.[10]

Although the initial legislative session was brief, several personnel changes occurred, most of them because members accepted other posts. Mason County elected Alexander D. Orr to the House, but then the electors sent him to the Senate. When he accepted the Senate post, the House issued a writ of election that resulted in his replacement by Arthur Fox on June 19. Another House writ was issued when the Committee on Privileges and Elections discovered that Thomas Clay of Madison County had not lived in the state long enough to be eligible. Haile Talbot replaced him on June 19. One Benjamin Frye may have started a well known Kentucky tradition for election losers; he petitioned the House to deny a seat to Joshua Hobbs of Nelson County because of alleged unfair election practices. His petition was rejected, and that also became a Kentucky political tradition. Another writ of election was issued for Lincoln County on June 27 when Henry Pawling accepted election to fill a Senate vacancy, and two others were authorized on June 29, the last day of the session. Robert Mosby (Mercer) had also accepted election to the Senate, and William Steele (Woodford) resigned when Shelby appointed him county surveyor.

Despite a much smaller membership than the House, the Senate also made several changes. John Logan (Lincoln) resigned on June 25 after having been elected treasurer by the General Assembly a week earlier. The Senate obtained an instant replacement by electing Henry Pawling, but his election was invalidated because the senators had neglected to take the prescribed oath for electors before voting. By then they had second thoughts, for instead of electing Pawling they chose James Knox. The selection of Senator William McDowell as State Auditor on June 28 resulted in his resignation the next day. Robert Mosby was elected to replace him.[11]

The revenue bill (Act 6) was without question one of the most important measures passed during the first session. Its scope would have a profound effect on the activities of the government. The constitution required that it originate in the House, and it received early attention there. An important decision was reached on June 7 when the representatives voted 27-8 that all revenue would have to be paid in specie; tobacco had often been the primary medium of exchange in the specie-

scarce frontier economy. In adjusting to the change, the legislators ruled that a pound of tobacco should be considered
equal to one penny. The revenue bill went to the Senate on June
21, received approval there, and was signed by the governor on
June 26. The major source of revenue was a tax placed on land,
slaves, and livestock. The annual tax on 100 acres of land was
two shillings. (Since a British pound was reckoned equal to
$3.33, a shilling was worth 16⅔ cents.) Slaves were also taxed
at two shillings, except for exemptions allowed by the county
court for age and infirmity. Horses, mares, colts, and mules
were taxed at eight pence each, but a stud's tax was the same as
the fee received for covering a mare. The cattle tax was three
pence each. Agricultural vehicles were exempt, but other
means of locomotion were taxed at either four or six shillings
per wheel. Each ordinary (tavern) had to have a license that
cost ten pounds annually, and retail stores paid at the same
rate. A "sin" tax of ten pounds was placed on billiard tables.
Complicated levies on legal papers ranged from three to
twelve shillings. Since little revenue would be collected in the
near future, the act authorized the treasurer to borrow up to
£2,000 at 5 percent interest to pay the operating costs of the
government.[12]

Establishing a court system required considerable time
and attention, and the two measures (Acts 35 and 36) that set
up the system did not become law until June 28. The constitution had mandated the Court of Appeals as the state's supreme
court, but the General Assembly had to fill in the details. The
decision was to have a three-judge court, headed by the chief
justice of Kentucky, that would hold two annual sessions. Its
jurisdiction was largely appellate, the major exception being
the controversial constitutional provision that it have original
and final jurisdiction in land cases. An effort in the Senate to
remove the original jurisdiction failed; it was not removed
until 1795. Based on population estimates, counties were allocated eight to sixteen justices of the peace. Any three of them
constituted a county court, but most or all of the justices sat to
hear important cases. Judgments were final if the value of the
suit did not exceed fifty shillings or 500 pounds of tobacco; if

the value was greater, an appeal could go to the quarter sessions court. In a clear violation of the principle of separation of powers, the county court also had a number of administrative powers. Historian Robert Ireland asserted that "in many ways the county courts were the most vital part of Kentucky government" for it was the level of government with which citizens were most likely to become involved. But in Kentucky the county courts lost some important powers they had enjoyed under Virginia law. They could not fill vacancies in their ranks or appoint sheriffs, other county officials, and militia officers, and they no longer doubled as the judges on the quarter sessions courts. Justices of the peace who sat on the quarter sessions courts were not allowed to serve on the county courts as well.

The quarter sessions courts heard more important cases, including criminal cases where the possible penalty extended to loss of life or limb. The Court of Oyer and Terminer had three judges appointed by the governor and confirmed by the Senate. Meeting in two annual sessions, it heard the more serious criminal cases. No appeal could be made or writ of error obtained from its decisions. George Muter was the first head of this court.[13]

Most of the acts passed during the first session concerned various aspects of the state government although much time was spent on an Act (25) concerning stray animals. Acts 18, 19, and 28, for example, dealt with the militia. Act 1 established the office of state auditor, Act 20 provided for a surveyor in each county, and Act 31 authorized the appointment of tax commissioners. Act 27 allowed payment to the members and employees of the constitutional convention; Act 34 arranged payment to Mr. Bradford, the public printer; and Act 37 provided the authority to pay the members of the General Assembly and its employees. The two speakers received $3.00 per day, and the other members got $1.00. Travel time was included, and the legislators decided that under existing conditions twenty-five miles would constitute a day. The clerks of the houses were voted $50.00 per week; the committee clerks received between $11.00 and $14.00 weekly; the sergeants-at-arms got $14.00 and the doorkeepers $8.00 weekly. Chaplain Gano was voted $10.00 after an unsuccessful protest that ministers should not be paid anything by the state.[14]

Four new counties were created during the session despite some petitions against the divisions. Washington was carved out of Nelson County, Scott out of Woodford, Shelby out of Jefferson, and Logan out of Lincoln (Acts 2, 3, 9, and 12). Several other acts were also concerned with local government. A town was authorized at Woodford Courthouse (Act 10), Bardstown (Act 21) and Paris (Act 22) received attention, and the appointment of a sheriff was approved for Lincoln County (Act 15). Acts 5, 7, and 17 concerned relations with the national government. Kentucky was entitled to two representatives in Congress, and Act 5 created two districts, divided by the Kentucky River, for their election. The second presidential election would be held later in 1792, so Act 7 established four districts for the election of electors. The Bill of Rights had already been added to the federal Constitution, but in Act 17 the General Assembly gave Kentucky's endorsement, including the two proposed amendments that had not been ratified by the other states. The General Assembly received numerous private requests and petitions, most of which it ignored or rejected. Acts 13, 14, 22, and 26 were private bills that won approval. Some members of the first General Assembly must have had previous legislative experience, for they employed the classic technique of dealing with some problems by postponing them to the next session.[15]

On June 18 the House and Senate took care of two joint elections for which they were responsible. John Brown, John Edwards, and Robert Breckinridge were nominated for United States senator; Brown and Edwards were elected. The constitution had given the selection of the state treasurer to the legislature instead of the governor, and on the same day the two houses proceeded to that election. Six men were nominated, and Senator John Logan was chosen. In neither instance did the journals give the vote.[16]

On that busy Monday, June 18, the House of Representatives started the complicated process mandated by the constitution for the selection of a site for the state capital. The House elected twenty-one prospective members of a site committee. Two days later the House members from Fayette and Mercer counties alternately struck names from the panel until only five remained. Robert Todd (Fayette), John Edwards (Bourbon), John Allen (Bourbon), Thomas Kennedy (Madison), and Henry Lee (Mason) became the site commissioners. During the next few months they received proposals from a number of potential locations: Frankfort, Leestown, Ledgerwood's Bend in Mercer County, a tract at Delany's Ferry in Woodford County, Louisville, Lexington, Petersburg in Woodford County, and Boonesboro. The commissioners began visiting the possible sites in early August 1792 and made their recommendation in December. Since the new government had limited resources, the inducements offered on behalf of the various locations had a significant impact on the committee's decision. Andrew Holmes, who had purchased a considerable part of Frankfort from James Wilkinson in early 1792, led the citizens of that community in making the most comprehensive and attractive offer.

Holmes started by offering to donate the use for seven years of the house built by Wilkinson, eight choice town lots designated as public on the town plot, approximately half of the unsold lots, and the rents for seven years from a warehouse located on the bank of the Kentucky River. Upon reasonable notice, Holmes also promised to supply many of the materials needed for the construction of one or more public buildings: ten boxes of 10 × 12-inch glass, 1,500 pounds of nails, £50 worth of locks and hinges, ample supplies of stone, and timber. More lots would be laid off if needed. In addition to Holmes's inducements, eight other citizens, headed by Harry Innes, pledged $3,000 in specie if Frankfort was selected. A group at Boonesboro made a strong bid of 18,550 acres and £2,630 in specie, but the Frankfort offer was too good to be refused. Frankfort also had a decided advantage in location. Much of the controversy over the selection centered on whether the capital would be north or south of the Kentucky River. Frankfort hugged the river, and, while it was on the north bank, its future growth was almost certain to extend to the south side. Frankfort had a more central location than Boonesboro, and that also influenced the choice. On December 5, 1792, the commissioners recommended Frankfort to the General Assembly, and three days later the legislature accepted their proposal. When the legislature adjourned on December 22 it was "to hold its next session in the house of Andrew Holmes, at Frankfort on the Kentucky River."[17]

But the selection of the capital lay in the future as the General Assembly ended its first session on June 29, 1792. The legislature generously offered the auditor, treasurer, and land registrar the use of their building until the next session. Then the General Assembly adjourned until the first Monday in November.

Kentucky had achieved statehood, had drafted a constitution, and had put it into effect. The long road to statehood had at last been covered. Where the road of statehood would lead in the future was uncertain. It would depend upon many factors, not the least of which was the will and determination of Kentuckians.

APPENDIX A

Formation of Counties
1780-1792

New County	County from Which Formed	Year
1. Jefferson	Kentucky (Virginia)	1780
2. Fayette	Kentucky (Virginia)	1780
3. Lincoln	Kentucky (Virginia)	1780
4. Nelson	Jefferson	1784
5. Bourbon	Fayette	1785
6. Mercer	Lincoln	1785
7. Madison	Lincoln	1785
8. Mason	Bourbon	1788
9. Woodford	Fayette	1788
10. Washington	Nelson	1792
11. Scott	Woodford	1792
12. Shelby	Jefferson	1792
13. Logan	Lincoln	1792
14. Clark	Fayette, Bourbon	1792
15. Hardin	Nelson	1792
16. Green	Lincoln, Nelson	1792

APPENDIX B

Chronology
Major Events on the Road to Statehood

1776		Kentucky County created
1779		Basic Virginia land laws passed
1780		Lincoln, Jefferson, and Fayette counties created
		Kentucky County becomes District of Kentucky
1782		Supreme court set up for District of Kentucky
1784		Nelson County created
		Spain closes Mississippi River to Americans
	Dec. 27	First Convention meets
1785		Bourbon, Madison, and Mercer counties created
	May 23	Second Convention meets
	Aug. 8	Third Convention meets
1786	Jan. 16	First Enabling Act
	Sept.	Fourth Convention lacks quorum
1787	Jan.	Fourth Convention meets
	Jan. 10	Second Enabling Act
	April	Wilkinson leaves on first trip to New Orleans
	Aug. 11	First issue of *Kentucke Gazette* appears
	Aug. 22	Wilkinson's First Memorial
	Sept. 17	Fifth Convention meets
1788		Woodford and Mason counties created
	June 25	Virginia ratifies federal constitution
	July 3	Articles of Confederation; Congress defers admission of Kentucky to new government
	July 29	Sixth Convention meets

	Nov. 4	Seventh Convention meets
	Dec. 29	Third Enabling Act
1789		Federal district court established
	March	Spain opens Mississippi River to trade upon payment of tax
	June 5	Wilkinson leaves on second trip to New Orleans
	July 20	Eighth Convention meets
	Sept. 17	Wilkinson's Second Memorial
	Dec. 18	Fourth Enabling Act
1790	July 26	Ninth Convention meets
1791		Wilkinson secures army commission, leaves Kentucky
1792	April 2	Tenth Convention meets, adopts constitution
	May 1	General election held
	May 15	Electors elect Isaac Shelby as governor and eleven senators
	June 1	Kentucky becomes fifteenth state in the Union
	June 4	General Assembly opens first session
		Isaac Shelby inaugurated governor

APPENDIX C

The Kentucky Constitution of 1792

We, the representatives of the people of the State of Kentucky, in Convention assembled, do ordain and establish this Constitution for its government.

ARTICLE I.

SEC. 1. The powers of government shall be divided into three distinct departments, each of them to be confided to a separate body of magistracy, to-wit: those which are legislative to one, those which are executive to another, and those which are judiciary to another.

SEC. 2. No person, or collection of persons, being of one of these departments, shall exercise any power properly belonging to either of the others, except in the instances hereinafter expressly permitted.

SEC. 3. The legislative power of this Commonwealth shall be vested in a General Assembly, which shall consist of a Senate and House of Representatives.

SEC. 4. The Representatives shall be chosen annually, by the qualified electors of each county respectively, on the first Tuesday in May; but the several elections may be continued for three days, if, in the opinion of the presiding officer or officers, it shall be necessary, and no longer.

SEC. 5. No person shall be a Representative who shall not have attained the age of twenty-four years, and have been a citizen and inhabitant of the State two years next preceding his election, and the last six months thereof an inhabitant of the county in which he may be chosen, unless he shall have been absent on the public business of the United States or of this State.

SEC. 6. Within two years after the first meeting of the General Assembly, and within every subsequent term of four years, an enumeration of the free male inhabitants above twenty-one years of age shall be made, in such manner as may be directed by law. The number of Representatives shall, at the several periods of making such enumeration, be fixed by the Legislature, and apportioned among the several counties according to the number of free male inhabitants above the age of twenty-one years in each, and shall never be less than forty nor greater than one hundred; but no county hereafter erected shall be entitled to a separate representation, until a sufficient number of male inhabitants above the age of twenty-one years, shall be contained within it, to entitle them to one Representative agreeable to the ratio which shall then be established.

SEC. 7. The Senators shall be chosen for four years.

SEC. 8. Until the first enumeration be made, the Senate shall consist of eleven members, and thereafter for every four members added to the House of Representatives, one member shall be added to the Senate.

SEC. 9. In choosing the Senate, one member at least shall be elected from each county, until the number of counties is equal to the number of Senators; after which, when a new county is made, it shall, as to the choice of Senators, be considered as being a part of the county or counties from which it shall have been taken.

SEC. 10. The Senate shall be chosen in the following manner: All persons qualified to vote for Representatives shall, on the first Tuesday in May, in the present year, and on the same day in every fourth year forever thereafter, at the place appointed by law for choosing Representatives, elect by ballot, by a majority of votes, as many persons as they are entitled to have for Representatives for their respective counties, to be electors of the Senate.

SEC. 11. No person shall be chosen an elector who shall not have resided in the State three years next before his election, and who shall not have attained the age of twenty-seven years.

SEC. 12. The electors of the Senate shall meet at such place as shall be appointed for convening the Legislature, on the third Tuesday in May in the present year, and on the same day in every fourth year forever thereafter; and they, or a majority of them, so met, shall proceed to elect, by ballot, as Senators, men of the most wisdom, experience and virtue, above twenty-seven years of age, who shall have been residents of the State above two whole years next preceding the election. If on the ballot two or more persons shall have an equal number of ballots in their favor, by which the choice shall not be determined by the first ballot, then the electors shall again ballot before they separate, in which they shall be confined to the persons who, on the first ballot, shall have an equal number, and they who shall have the greatest number in their favor on a second ballot, shall be accordingly declared and returned duly elected; and if, on the second ballot, an equal number shall still be in favor of two or more persons, then the election shall be determined by lot between those who have equal numbers; which proceedings of the electors shall be certified under their hands, and returned to the secretary for the time being, to whom shall also be made by the proper officers, returns of the persons chosen as electors in the respective counties.

SEC. 13. The electors of Senators shall judge of the qualifications and elections of members of their own body; and on a contested election, shall admit to a seat, as an elector, such qualified person as shall appear to them to have the greatest number of legal votes in his favor.

SEC. 14. The electors, immediately on their meeting, and before they proceed to the election of Senators, shall take an oath, or make affirmation of fidelity to this State, and also an oath or affirmation to elect without favor, affection, partiality, or prejudice, such person for Governor, and such persons for Senators, as they, in their judgment and conscience, believe best qualified for the respective offices.

SEC. 15. That in case of refusal, death, resignation, disqualification, or removal out of this State of any Senator, the Senate shall immediately thereupon, or at their next meeting thereafter, elect, by ballot, in the same manner as the electors are herein directed to choose Senators, another person in his place, for the residue of the said term of four years.

SEC. 16. The General Assembly shall meet on the first Monday in November, in every year, till the time of their meeting shall be altered by the Legislature, unless sooner convened by the Governor.

SEC. 17. Each House shall choose its Speaker and other officers, and the Senate shall also choose a speaker *pro tempore*, when their Speaker shall exercise the office of Governor.

SEC. 18. Each House shall judge of the qualifications of its members; contested elections shall be determined by a committee to be selected, formed, and regulated in such manner as shall be directed by law. A majority of each House shall constitute a quorum to do business, but a smaller number may adjourn from day to day, and may be authorized by law to compel the attendance of absent members, in such manner, and under such penalties, as may be provided.

SEC. 19. Each House may determine the rules of its proceedings, punish its members for disorderly behavior, and with the concurrence of two-thirds, expel a member; but not a second time for the same cause.

SEC. 20. Each House shall keep a journal of its proceedings, and publish them weekly, except such parts of them as may require secrecy; and the yeas and nays of the members on any question shall, at the desire of any two of them, be entered on the journals.

SEC. 21. The doors of each House, and of committees of the whole, shall be open, unless when the business shall be such as ought to be kept secret.

SEC. 22. Neither House shall, without the consent of the other, adjourn for more than three days; nor to any other place than that in which the two Houses shall be sitting.

SEC. 23. The members of the General Assembly, and the electors of the Senate, shall receive from the public treasury a compensation for their services, which, for the present, shall be six shillings a day during their attendance on, going to, and returning from the Legislature, and the place for choosing the Senators; but the same may be increased or diminished by law, if circumstances shall require it, but no alteration shall be made, to take effect during the existence of the Legislature which shall make such alteration. They shall, in all cases, except treason, felony, breach or surety of the peace, be privileged from arrest during their attendance at the session of the respective Houses, and at the place for choosing Senators, and in going to and returning from the same; and for any speech or debate in either House, they shall not be questioned in any other place.

SEC. 24. No Senator or Representative shall, during the time for which he shall have been elected, or for one year afterward, be appointed to any civil office under this State, which shall have been created, or the emoluments of which shall have been increased, during the time such Senator or Representative was in office: *Provided,* That no member of the first Legislature, which shall be assembled under this Constitution, shall be precluded from being appointed to any office which may have been created during his time of service in the said Legislature; and no minister of religious societies, member of Congress or other person holding any office of profit under the United States or this Commonwealth, except attorneys at law, justices of the peace, militia officers, and coroners, shall be a member of either House during his continuance to act as a minister, in Congress or in office.

SEC. 25. When vacancies happen in the House of Representatives, the Speaker shall issue writs of election to fill such vacancies.

SEC. 26. All bills for raising revenue shall originate in the House of Representatives; but the Senate may propose amendments as in other bills.

SEC. 27. Each Senator, Representative, and sheriff shall, before he be permitted to act as such, take an oath or make affirmation that he hath not, directly or indirectly, given or promised any bribe or treat to procure his election to the said office; and every person shall be disqualified from serving as a Senator, Representative, or sheriff for the term for which he shall have been elected, who shall be convicted of having given or offered any bribe or treat, or canvassed for the said office.

SEC. 28. Every bill which shall have passed both Houses shall be presented to the Governor; if he approve, he shall sign it; but if he shall not approve, he shall return it, with his objections, to the House in which it shall have originated, who shall enter the objections at large upon their journals, and proceed to reconsider it; if, after such reconsideration, two-thirds of that House shall agree to pass the bill, it shall be sent, with the objections, to the other House, by which it shall likewise be reconsidered; and if approved by two-thirds of that House, it shall be a law; but, in such cases, the votes of both Houses shall be determined by yeas and nays, and the names of the persons voting for or against the bill shall be entered on the journals of each House, respectively; if any bill shall not be returned by the Governor within ten days (Sundays excepted) after it shall have been presented to him, it shall be a law in like manner as if he had signed it, unless the General Assembly, by their adjournment, prevent its return; in which case it shall be a law unless sent back within three days after their next meeting.

SEC. 29. Every order, resolution, or vote, to which the concurrence of both Houses may be necessary, except on a question of adjournment, shall be presented to the Governor, and before it shall take effect, be approved by him; or being disapproved, shall be repassed by two-thirds of both Houses, according to the rules and limitations prescribed in case of a bill.

ARTICLE II.

SEC. 1. The supreme executive power of this Commonwealth shall be vested in a Governor.

SEC. 2. The Governor shall be chosen by the electors of the Senate at the same time, at the same place, and in the same manner, that they are herein directed to elect Senators; and the said electors shall make return of their proceedings in the choice of a Governor, to the Secretary for the time being.

SEC. 3. The Governor shall hold his office during four years from the first day of June next ensuing his election.

SEC. 4. He shall be at least thirty years of age, and have been a citizen and inhabitant of this State at least two years next before his election, unless he shall have been absent on the public business of the United States or of this State.

SEC. 5. No member of Congress, or person holding any office under the United States or this State, shall exercise the office of Governor.

SEC. 6. The Governor shall, at stated times, receive for his services a compensation, which shall neither be increased nor diminished during the period for which he shall have been elected.

SEC. 7. He shall be commander-in-chief of the army and navy of this Commonwealth, and of the militia, except when they shall be called into the service of the United States.

SEC. 8. He shall nominate, and by and with the advice and consent of the Senate, appoint all officers whose offices are established by this Constitution, or shall be established by law, and who appointments are not herein otherwise provided for; but no person shall be appointed to an office within any county, who shall not have been a citizen and inhabitant therein one year next before his appointment, if the county shall have been so long erected; but, if it shall not have been so long erected, then within the limits of the county or counties out of which it shall have been taken.

SEC. 9. The Governor shall have power to fill up all vacancies that may happen during the recess of the Senate, by granting commissions which shall expire at the end of their next session.

SEC. 10. He shall have power to remit fines and forfeitures, and grant reprieves and pardons, except in cases of impeachment; in cases of treason, he shall have power to grant reprieves until the end of the next session of the General Assembly, in whom the power of pardoning shall be vested.

SEC. 11. He may require information in writing from the officers in the executive department upon any subject relating to the duties of their respective offices.

SEC. 12. He shall, from time to time, give to the General Assembly information of the state of the Commonwealth, and recommend to their consideration such measures as he shall judge expedient.

Sec. 13. He may, on extraordinary occasions, convene the General Assembly, and in case of disagreement between the two Houses with respect to the time of adjournment, adjourn them to such time as he shall think proper, not exceeding four months.

Sec. 14. He shall take care that the laws be faithfully executed.

Sec. 15. In case of the death or resignation of the Governor, or of his removal from office, the Speaker of the Senate shall exercise the office of Governor until another shall be duly qualified.

Sec. 16. An Attorney General shall be appointed and commissioned during good behavior; he shall appear for the Commonwealth in all criminal prosecutions, and in all civil cases in which the Commonwealth shall be interested, in any of the superior courts; shall give his opinion when called upon for that purpose, by either branch of the Legislature, or by the Executive, and shall perform such other duties as shall be enjoined him by law.

Sec. 17. A Secretary shall be appointed and commissioned during the Governor's continuance in office, if he shall so long behave himself well; he shall keep a fair register of, and attest all the official acts and proceedings of the Governor, and shall, when required, lay the same and all papers, minutes and vouchers relative thereto, before either branch of the Legislature, and shall perform such other duties as shall be enjoined him by law.

ARTICLE III.

Sec. 1. In elections by the citizens, all free male citizens of the age of twenty-one years, having resided in the State two years, or the county in which they offer to vote one year next before the election, shall enjoy the rights of an elector; but no person shall be entitled to vote except in the county in which he shall actually reside at the time of the election.

Sec. 2. All elections shall be by ballot.

Sec. 3. Electors shall, in all cases, except treason, felony and breach or surety of the peace, be privileged from arrest during their attendance at elections, and in going to and returning from them.

ARTICLE IV.

Sec. 1. The House of Representatives shall have the sole power of impeaching.

SEC. 2. All impeachments shall be tried by the Senate; when setting for that purpose, the Senators shall be upon oath or affirmation; no person shall be convicted without the concurrence of two-thirds of the members present.

SEC. 3. The Governor and all other civil officers shall be liable to impeachment for any misdemeanor in office; but judgment in such cases shall not extend further than to removal from office and disqualification to hold any office of honor, trust or profit under this Commonwealth; but the party convicted shall, nevertheless, be liable and subject to indictment, trial and punishment according to law.

ARTICLE V.

SEC. 1. The judicial power of this Commonwealth, both as to matters of law and equity, shall be vested in one supreme court, which shall be styled the Court of Appeals, and in such inferior courts as the Legislature may, from time to time, ordain and establish.

SEC. 2. The judges, both of the supreme and inferior courts, shall hold their offices during good behavior; but for any reasonable cause which shall not be sufficient ground of impeachment, the Governor may remove any of them on the address of two-thirds of each branch of the Legislature. They shall, at stated times, receive for their services an adequate compensation, to be fixed by law, which shall not be diminished during their continuance in office.

SEC. 3. The Supreme Court shall have original and final jurisdiction in all cases respecting the titles to land under the present land laws of Virginia, including those which may be depending in the present Supreme Court for the district of Kentucky, at the time of establishing of the said Supreme Court; and in all cases concerning contracts for land, prior to the establishing of those titles. And the said court shall have power to hear and determine the same in a summary way, and to direct the mode of bringing the same to a hearing, so as to enable them to do right and justice to the parties, with as little delay and at as small an expense as the nature of the business will allow; but the said court shall, in all such cases, oblige the parties to state the material parts of their complaint and defense in writing; and shall, on the conclusion of every cause, state on the records the whole merits of the case, the questions arising therefrom, the opinions of the court thereupon, and a summary of the reasons in support of those opinions.

SEC. 4. And it shall be the duty of each judge of the Supreme

Court, present at the hearing of such cause, and differing from a majority of the court, to deliver his opinion in writing, to be entered as aforesaid; and each judge shall deliver his opinion in open court. And the said court shall have power, on the determination of any such case, to award the legal costs against either party or to divide the same among the different parties, as to them shall seem just and right. And the said court shall have full power to take such steps as they may judge proper, to perpetuate testimony in all cases concerning such titles: *Provided,* That a jury shall always be empaneled for the finding of such facts as are not agreed by the parties; unless the parties, or their attorneys, shall waive their right of trial by a jury, and refer the matter of fact to the decision of the court: *Provided also,* That the Legislature may, whenever they may judge it expedient, pass an act or acts to regulate the mode of proceedings in such cases, or to take away entirely the original jurisdiction hereby given to the said court in such cases.

SEC. 5. In all other cases the Supreme Court shall have appellate jurisdiction only, with such exceptions and under such regulations as the Legislature shall make; and the Legislature may, from time to time, vest in the Supreme and inferior courts, or either of them, such powers, both in law and equity, as they shall judge proper and necessary for the due administration of justice.

SEC. 6. A competent number of justices of the peace shall be appointed in each county; they shall be commissioned during good behavior, but may be removed on conviction of misbehavior in office, or of any infamous crime, or on the address of both Houses of the Legislature.

SEC. 7. The judges shall by virtue of their office be conservators of the peace throughout the State. The style of all process shall be, *"The Commonwealth of Kentucky;"* all prosecutions shall be carried on in the name and by the authority of the Commonwealth of Kentucky, and conclude against the peace and dignity of the same.

ARTICLE VI.

SEC. 1. Sheriffs and coroners shall, at the times and places of elections of Representatives, be chosen by the citizens of each county qualified to vote for Representatives. They shall hold their offices for three years, if they shall so long behave themselves well, and until a successor be duly qualified; but no person shall be twice chosen or appointed sheriff in any term of six years. Vacancies in either of the said offices shall be filled by a new appointment to be made by the Governor, to continue until the next general election, and until a successor shall be chosen and qualified as aforesaid.

SEC. 2. The free men of this Commonwealth shall be armed and disciplined for its defense. Those who conscientiously scruple to bear arms shall not be compelled to do so, but shall pay an equivalent for personal service.

SEC. 3. The field and staff officers of the militia shall be appointed by the Governor, except the battalion staff officers, who shall be appointed by the field officers of each batallion respectively.

SEC. 4. The officers of companies shall be chosen by the persons enrolled in the list of each company, and the whole shall be commissioned during good behavior, and during their residence in the bounds of the battalion or company to which they shall be appointed.

SEC. 5. Each court shall appoint its own clerk, who shall hold his office during good behavior; but no person shall be appointed clerk only *pro tempore*, who shall not produce to the court appointing him, a certificate from a majority of the judges of the Court of Appeals that he hath been examined by their clerk in their presence, and under their direction, and that they judge him to be well qualified to execute the office of clerk to any court of the same dignity with that for which he offers himself. They shall be removable for breach of good behavior, by the Court of Appeals only, who shall be judges of the fact as well as of the law; two-thirds of the members present must concur in the sentence.

SEC. 6. All commissions shall be in the name and by the authority of the State of Kentucky, and be sealed with the State seal, and signed by the Governor.

SEC. 7. The State Treasurer shall be appointed annually by the joint ballot of both Houses.

ARTICLE VII.

SEC. 1. Members of the General Assembly, and all officers, executive and judicial, before they enter upon the execution of their respective offices, shall take the following oath or affirmation: "I do solemnly swear (or affirm, as the case may be), that I will be faithful and true to the Commonwealth of Kentucky, so long as I continue a citizen thereof, and that I will faithfully execute, to the best of my abilities, the office of ———, according to law."

ARTICLE VIII.

SEC. 1. Treason against the Commonwealth shall consist only in levying war against it, or in adhering to its enemies, giving them aid and comfort. No person shall be convicted of treason, unless on the testimony of two witnesses to the same overt act, or on his own confession in open court.

SEC. 2. Laws shall be made to exclude from office and from suffrage, those who shall thereafter be convicted of bribery, perjury, forgery, or other high crimes or misdemeanors; the privilege of free suffrage shall be supported by laws regulating elections, and prohibiting under adequate penalties, all undue influence thereon from power, bribery, tumult, or other improper practices.

SEC. 3. No money shall be drawn from the Treasury but in consequence of appropriations made by law, nor shall any appropriations of money for the support of an army be made for a longer term than one year, and a regular statement and account of the receipts and expenditures of all public money shall be published annually.

SEC. 4. The Legislature shall direct by law, in what manner and in what courts, suits may be brought against the Commonwealth.

SEC. 5. The manner of administering an oath or affirmation shall be such as is most consistent with the conscience of the deponent, and shall be esteemed by the Legislature the most solemn appeal to God.

SEC. 6. All laws now in force in the State of Virginia, not [in]consistent with this Constitution, which are of a general nature, and not local to the eastern part of that State, shall be in force in this State until they shall be altered or repealed by the Legislature.

SEC. 7. The compact with the State of Virginia, subject to such alterations as may be made therein, agreeably to the mode prescribed by the said compact, shall be considered as a part of this Constitution.

ARTICLE IX.

The Legislature shall have no power to pass laws for the emancipation of slaves without the consent of their owners, or without paying their owners, previous to such emancipation, a full equivalent in money for the slaves so emancipated; they shall have no power to prevent emigrants to this State from bringing with them such persons as are deemed slaves by the laws of any one of the United States, so long as any person of the same age or description shall be continued in slavery by the laws of this State; that they shall pass laws to permit the owners of slaves to emancipate them, saving the rights of creditors, and preventing them from becoming a charge to the county in which they reside; they shall have full power to prevent slaves being brought into this State as merchandise; they shall have full power to prevent any slave being brought into this State from a foreign country, and to prevent those from being brought into this State who have been since the first day of January, one thousand seven hundred and eighty-nine, or may hereafter be imported into any of the United States from a foreign country. And they shall have full power to pass such laws as may be necessary, to oblige the owners of slaves to treat them with humanity, to provide for them necessary clothing and provisions, to abstain from all injuries to them extending to life or limb; and in case of their neglect or refusal to comply with the directions of such laws, to have such slave or slaves sold for the benefit of their owner or owners.

ARTICLE X.

SEC. 1. The place for the Seat of Government shall be fixed in the following manner: The House of Representatives shall, during their session, which shall be held in the year one thousand seven hundred and ninety-two, choose, by ballot, twenty-one persons, from whom the representation from Mercer and Fayette counties then present shall alternately strike out one, until the number shall be reduced to five, who, or any three of them concurring in opinion, shall have power to fix on the place for the Seat of Government; to receive grants from individuals therefor, and to make such conditions with the proprietor or proprietors of the land so pitched on by them, as to them shall seem right and shall be agreed to by the said proprietor or proprietors, and lay off a town thereon in such manner as they shall judge most proper.

SEC. 2. The General Assembly and the Supreme Courts shall, within five years, hold their sessions at the place so pitched upon by the said commissioners; and the Seat of Government so fixed shall continue until it shall be changed by two-thirds of both branches of the Legislature. The commissioners, before they proceed to act, shall take an oath or make affirmation that they will discharge the trust reposed in them, in such manner as in their judgment will be most beneficial to the State at large.

ARTICLE XI.

SEC. 1. That the citizens of this State may have an opportunity to amend or change this Constitution in a peaceable manner, if to them it shall seem expedient, the persons qualified to vote for Representatives shall, at the general election to be held in the year one thousand seven hundred and ninety-seven, vote also by ballot, for or against a convention, as they shall severally choose to do; and if thereupon it shall appear that a majority of all the citizens in the State voting for Representatives have voted for a convention, the General Assembly shall direct that a similar ballot shall be taken the next year; and if, thereupon, it shall also appear that a majority of all the citizens of the State voting for Representatives have voted for a convention, the General Assembly shall, at their next session, call a convention, to consist of as many members as there shall be in the House of Representatives, to be chosen in the same manner, at the same places, and at the same time that Representatives are, by the citizens entitled to vote for Representatives, and to meet within three months after the said election, for the purpose of readopting, amending or changing this Constitution. If it shall appear upon the ballot of either year, that a majority of the citizens voting for Representatives is not in favor of a convention being called, it shall not be done until two-thirds of both branches of the Legislature shall deem it expedient.

ARTICLE XII.

That the general, great and essential principles of liberty and free government may be recognized and established, WE DECLARE——

SEC. 1. That all men, when they form a social compact, are equal, and that no man or set of men are entitled to exclusive separate public emoluments or privileges from the community, but in consideration of public services.

SEC. 2. That all power is inherent in the people, and all free governments are founded on their authority, and instituted for their peace, safety and happiness. For the advancement of these ends, they have at all times an unalienable and indefeasible right to alter, reform, or abolish their government, in such manner as they may think proper.

SEC. 3. That all men have a natural and indefeasible right to worship Almighty God according to the dictates of their own consciences; that no man can of right be compelled to attend, erect, or support any place of worship, or to maintain any ministry against his consent; that no human authority can, in any case whatever, control or interfere with the rights of conscience; and that no preference shall ever be given by law to any religious societies or modes of worship.

SEC. 4. That the civil rights, privileges or capacities of any citizen shall in nowise be diminished or enlarged on account of his religion.

SEC. 5. That all elections shall be free and equal.

SEC. 6. That trial by jury shall be as heretofore, and the right thereof remain inviolate.

SEC. 7. That printing-presses shall be free to every person who undertakes to examine the proceedings of the Legislature or any branch of Government; and no law shall ever be made to restrain the right thereof; the free communication of thoughts and opinions is one of the invaluable rights of man, and every citizen may freely speak, write, and print on any subject, being responsible for the abuse of that liberty.

SEC. 8. In prosecutions for the publication of papers investigating the official conduct of officers or men in a public capacity, or where the matter published is proper for public information, the truth thereof may be given in evidence. And in all indictments for libels, the jury shall have a right to determine the law and the facts under the direction of the court as in other cases.

SEC. 9. That the people shall be secure in their persons, houses, papers and possessions from unreasonable seizures and searches; and that no warrant to search any place or to seize any person or things shall issue without describing them as nearly as may be, nor without probable cause, supported by oath or affirmation.

SEC. 10. That in all criminal prosecutions, the accused hath a right to be heard by himself and his counsel; to demand the nature and cause of the accusation against him, to meet the witnesses face to face; to have compulsory process for obtaining witnesses in his favor; and in prosecutions by indictment or information, a speedy public trial by an impartial jury of the vicinage; that he can not be compelled to give evidence against himself, nor can he be deprived of his life, liberty or property, unless by the judgment of his peers, or the law of the land.

SEC. 11. That no person shall, for any indictable offense, be proceeded against criminally by information; except in cases arising in the land or naval forces, or in the militia when in actual service, in time of war or public danger, or by leave of the court for oppression or misdemeanor in office.

SEC. 12. No person shall, for the same offense, be twice put in jeopardy of his life or limb; nor shall any man's property be taken or applied to public use without the consent of his representatives, and without just compensation being previously made to him.

SEC. 13. That all courts shall be open, and every person for an injury done him in his lands, goods, person or reputation, shall have remedy by the due course of law; and right and justice administered without sale, denial or delay.

SEC. 14. That no power of suspending laws shall be exercised, unless by the Legislature or its authority.

SEC. 15. That excessive bail shall not be required, nor excessive fines imposed, nor cruel punishment inflicted.

SEC. 16. That all prisoners shall be bailable by sufficient sureties, unless for capital offenses when the proof is evident or presumption great; and the privilege of the writ of habeas corpus shall not be suspended, unless when in cases of rebellion or invasion, the public safety may require it.

SEC. 17. That the person of a debtor, where there is not strong presumption of fraud, shall not be continued in prison after delivering up his estate for the benefit of his creditors, in such manner as shall be prescribed by law.

SEC. 18. That no *ex post facto* law, nor any law impairing contracts, shall be made.

SEC. 19. That no person shall be attained of treason or felony by the Legislature.

SEC. 20. That no attainder shall work corruption of blood, nor, except during the life of the offender, forfeiture of estate to the Commonwealth.

SEC. 21. The estates of such person as shall destroy their own lives shall descend or vest as in case of natural death, and if any person shall be killed by casualty, there shall be no forfeiture by reason thereof.

SEC. 22. That the citizens have a right, in a peaceable manner, to assemble together for their common good, and to apply to those invested with the powers of government for redress of grievances or other proper purposes by petition, address or remonstrance.

SEC. 23. The rights of the citizens to bear arms in defense of themselves and the State shall not be questioned.

SEC. 24. That no standing army shall, in time of peace, be kept up without the consent of the Legislature; and the military shall, in all cases and at all times, be in strict subordination to the civil power.

SEC. 25. That no soldier shall, in time of peace, be quartered in any house, without the consent of the owner, nor in time of war, but in a manner to be prescribed by law.

SEC. 26. That the Legislature shall not grant any title of nobility or hereditary distinction, nor create any office the appointment of which shall be for a longer time than during good behavior.

SEC. 27. That emigration from the State shall not be prohibited.

SEC. 28. To guard against transgressions of the high powers which we have delegated, WE DECLARE, that everything in this article is excepted out of the general powers of government, and shall forever remain inviolate; and that all laws contrary thereto, or contrary to this Constitution shall be void.

SCHEDULE.

That no inconvenience may arise from the establishing the government of this State, and in order to carry the same into complete operation, it is hereby declared and ordained:

SEC. 1. That all rights, actions, prosecutions, claims, and contracts, as well of individuals, as of bodies corporate, shall continue as if the said government had not been established.

SEC. 2. That all officers, civil and military, now in commission under the State of Virginia, shall continue to hold and exercise their offices until the 10th day of August next, and no longer.

SEC. 3. That until the first enumeration shall be made as directed by the sixth section of the first article of this Constitution, the county of Jefferson shall be entitled to elect three Representatives; the county of Lincoln, four Representatives; the county of Fayette, nine Representatives; the county of Nelson, six Representatives; the county of Mercer, four Representatives; the county of Madison, three Representatives; the county of Bourbon, five Representatives; the county of Woodford, four Representatives; and the county of Mason, two Representatives.

SEC. 4. The General Assembly shall meet at Lexington on the fourth day of June next.

SEC. 5. All returns herein directed to be made to the Secretary shall, previously to his appointment, be made to the clerk of the Supreme Court for the district of Kentucky.

SEC. 6. Until a seal shall be procured for the State, the Governor shall be at liberty to use his private seal.

SEC. 7. The oaths of office herein directed to be taken may be administered by any justice of the peace, until the Legislature shall otherwise direct.

SEC. 8. All bonds given by any officer within the district of Kentucky, payable to the Governor of Virginia, may be prosecuted in the name of the Governor of Kentucky.

SEC. 9. All offenses against the laws of Virginia, which have been committed within the present district of Kentucky, or which may be committed within the same before the first day of June next, shall be cognizable in the courts of this State, in the same manner that they would be if they were committed within this State after the said first day of June.

SEC. 10. At the elections herein directed to be held in May next, the sheriff of each county, or in case of his absence, one of his deputies, shall preside, and if they neglect or refuse to act, the said election shall be held by any one of the justices of the peace for the county where such refusal or neglect shall happen; each officer holding such election having first taken an oath before a justice of the peace to conduct the said election with impartiality, shall have power to administer to any person offering to vote at such election, the following oath or affirmation: "I do swear (or affirm) that I am qualified to vote for Representatives in the county of _____ agreeably to the Constitution formed for the State of Kentucky;" and such officer shall have a right to refuse to receive the vote of any person who shall refuse to take the said oath, or make affirmation when tendered to him; and the said elections shall be held at the several places appointed for holding courts in the different counties.

SEC. 11. The Government of the Commonwealth of Kentucky shall commence on the first day of June next.

Done in Convention at Danville, the nineteenth day of April, one thousand seven hundred and ninety-two, and of the independence of the United States of America, the sixteenth.

By order of the Convention.

SAMUEL M'DOWELL, *P. C.*

Attest: THOMAS TODD, *C. C.*

Notes

These short forms have been used:

FCHQ: *The Filson Club History Quarterly*
Register: *Register of the Kentucky Historical Society*

1. STIRRINGS OF DISCONTENT

1. "Memoir," in James Alton James, ed., *George Rogers Clark Papers*, 2 vols. (Springfield, Ill., 1912-26), 1:209.

2. Ibid., 213; Temple Bodley, *George Rogers Clark: His Life and Public Service* (Boston, 1926), 29-32.

3. William Hayden English, *Conquest of the Country Northwest of the River Ohio, 1778-1783, and Life of Gen. George Rogers Clark*, 2 vols. (Indianapolis, 1906), 1:73-75, 461-63.

4. William Littell, comp., *Statute Law of Kentucky*, 5 vols. (Frankfort, 1809-19), 1:viii. William Stewart Lester, *The Transylvania Colony* (Spencer, Ind., 1935), is a detailed account, although somewhat anti-Henderson.

5. Arthur K. Moore, *The Frontier Mind: A Cultural Analysis of the Kentucky Frontiersman* (Lexington, 1957), 3.

6. Samuel Meredith, Jr., to John Breckinridge, March 2, 1791, Breckinridge Family Papers, Library of Congress (hereafter cited as Breckinridge Papers).

7. Samuel M. Wilson, *The First Land Court of Kentucky, 1779-1780* (Lexington, 1923), 49.

8. Lucien Beckner, ed., "Reverend John D. Shane's Interview with Pioneer William Clinkenbeard," *FCHQ* 2 (April 1928): 98.

9. Quotation in Temple Bodley, *Our First Great West* (Louisville, 1938), 117-18; Judge Charles Kerr, ed., William Elsey Connelley and E.M. Coulter, *History of Kentucky*, 5 vols. (Chicago, 1922), 1:288-89.

10. Thomas L. Purvis, "The Ethnic Descent of Kentucky's Early Population: A Statistical Investigation of European and American Sources of Immigration, 1790-1820," *Register* 80 (Summer 1982): 259-60; Theodore Roosevelt, *The Winning of the West*, 4 vols. (New York, 1889), 3:4-6, 16-17.

11. Lewis and Richard H. Collins, *History of Kentucky*, 2 vols. (Covington, Ky., 1874), 1:253-54. This portion of the "Outline History" was written by John A. McClung.

12. Temple Bodley, *History of Kentucky*, 4 vols. (Louisville, 1928), 1:347; Justin Winsor, *The Westward Movement* (Boston, 1897), 526.

13. Roosevelt, *Winning of the West*, 3:208.

14. Thomas Robson Hay, ed., "Letters of Mrs. Anne Wilkinson from Kentucky, 1788-1789," *Pennsylvania Magazine of History and Biography*" 56 (Jan. 1932): 52. Some punctuation has been added.

15. C.C. Todd, "The Early Courts of Kentucky," *Register* 3 (Sept. 1905): 33-35; Wilson, *First Land Court*, 22-24; Mary K. Bonsteel Tachau, *Federal Courts in the Early Republic: Kentucky, 1789-1816* (Princeton, N.J., 1978), 14-23; Robert M. Ireland, *The County Courts in Antebellum Kentucky* (Lexington, 1972), 7-17. Tachau's study is also the best account of Harry Innes's career.

16. Among the many discussions of this critical concern are: Neal O. Hammon, "Land Acquisition on the Kentucky Frontier," *Register* 78 (Autumn 1980): 297-321; idem, "Settlers, Land Jobbers, and Outlayers: A Quantitative Analysis of Land Acquisition on the Kentucky Frontier," *Register* 84 (Summer 1986): 241-62; R.S. Cotterill, *History of Pioneer Kentucky* (Cincinnati, 1917), 229-33; Patricia Watlington, *The Partisan Spirit: Kentucky Politics, 1779-1792* (New York, 1972), 1-26; and Thomas D. Clark, *Agrarian Kentucky* (Lexington, 1977), 4-9.

17. Mann Butler, *A History of the Commonwealth of Kentucky* (Louisville, 1834), 101; Joan Wells Coward, *Kentucky in the New Republic: The Process of Constitution Making* (Lexington, 1979), 4-5. Hereafter cited as *Kentucky Constitutions*.

18. William Wilson Hume Clay, "Kentucky: The Awful Path to Statehood" (Ph.D. diss., Univ. of Kentucky, 1966), 5.

19. Facsimile in English, *Conquest of Northwest*, 1:40-41; Walker Daniel to George Rogers Clark, Sept. 15, 1783, in James, *Clark Papers*, 2:246-47.

20. Jonathan Cowans to Levi Todd, Aug. 2, 1806, Draper Collection, 16 CC 41-42. The originals of the Draper Collection are at the Wisconsin Historical Society.

21. Thomas Paine, *The Public Good: Being An Examination into the Claim of Virginia to the Vacant Western Territory* (London, 1817; originally published Albany, N.Y., 1780); Kerr, ed., *History of Kentucky,* 1:222-24; Dumas Malone, *Jefferson and His Time,* 6 vols. (Boston, 1948-81), 1:335.

22. Humphrey Marshall, *The History of Kentucky* (Frankfort, 1812), 185-87; Kerr, ed., *History of Kentucky,* 1:224-25. Marshall did not publish a projected second volume in 1812; later he issued *The History of Kentucky,* 2 vols. (Frankfort, 1824). References to the 1824 edition will include a volume number.

23. July 12, 1785, quoted in Percy Willis Christian, "General James Wilkinson and Kentucky Separation, 1784-1798" (Ph.D. diss., Northwestern Univ., 1935), 31. Arthur P. Whitaker, *The Spanish-American Frontier: 1783-1795* (Boston, 1927), 92, 118, denies that the analogy was completely valid.

24. John Anthony Caruso, *The Appalachian Frontier* (Indianapolis, 1959), 150.

25. Wade Hall, ed., "A Long Wilderness Trail: A Young Lawyer's 1785 Letter from Danville, Kentucky, to Massachusetts," *FCHQ* 61 (July 1987): 290.

26. William Breckinridge to John Breckinridge, Feb. 5, 1785, Breckinridge Papers.

27. Charles Simms Papers, Library of Congress, quoted in Watlington, *Partisan Spirit,* 75.

28. Quoted in Peter S. Onuf, *Statehood and Union: A History of the Northwest Ordinance* (Bloomington, Ind., 1987), 29-30.

29. Tachau, *Federal Courts,* 169.

30. Herbert A. Johnson, ed., *Papers of John Marshall,* 5 vols. to date (Chapel Hill, N.C., 1974-), 1:133.

31. Speed to Governor Benjamin Harrison, May 22, 1784, *Calendar of Virginia State Papers,* 11 vols. (Richmond, Va., 1875-93), 3:589.

32. James R. Robertson, ed., *Petitions of the Early Inhabitants of Kentucky to the General Assembly of Virginia, 1769 to 1792* (Louisville, 1914), 67-68.

33. Whitaker, *Spanish-American Frontier,* 63-77; Richard B. Morris, *The Forging of the Union, 1781-1789* (New York, 1987), 234-44.

2. THE EARLY CONVENTIONS

1. Charles Gano Talbert, *Benjamin Logan: Kentucky Frontiersman* (Lexington, 1962), 140, 258; Marshall, *History of Kentucky,* 60-72.

2. John C. Doolan, "The Constitutions and Constitutional Conventions of 1792 and 1799," *Proceedings of the Sixteenth Annual Meeting of the Kentucky State Bar Association, July 5-6, 1917* (Louisville, 1918), 141.

3. Brooks to Arthur Campbell, Nov. 7, 1784, Draper Collection, 11 J 37-38; Marshall, *History of Kentucky,* 1:190-92; Caruso, *Appalachian Frontier,* 313.

4. Talbert, *Logan,* 195-97.

5. Cotterill, *Pioneer Kentucky,* 210-11.

6. General James Taylor, "Autobiography," Durrett Collection, Univ. of Chicago.

7. Watlington, *Partisan Spirit,* 35-64; Coward, *Kentucky Constitutions,* 7-9, 173n; Tachau, *Federal Courts,* 35-36. Dr. Watlington's fine study is the best guide to the politics of this era. We have had amiable disagreement on the subject of political parties. She believes they existed during this period; I contend that they were no more than political factions.

8. Reuben T. Durrett, *The Centenary of Kentucky* (Louisville, 1892), 51; Daniel to Harrison, May 21, 1784, *Calendar of Virginia State Papers,* 3:586-87; Richard J. Cox, ed., "'A Touch of Kentucky News & State of Politics': Two Letters of Levi Todd, 1784 and 1788," *Register* 76 (July 1978): 219.

9. Calvin Morgan Fackler, *Early Days in Danville* (Louisville, 1941), 1-35; Bodley, *History of Kentucky,* 1:341.

10. Thomas P. Abernethy, ed., "Journal of the First Kentucky Convention, Dec. 27, 1784-Jan. 5, 1785," *Journal of Southern History* 1 (Feb. 1935): 69-70.

11. Ibid., 71-72; Talbert, *Logan,* 197-98.

12. Abernethy, ed., "Journal of First Convention," 72-73.

13. Ibid., 74.

14. Ibid., 75-76.

15. Ibid., 77.

16. Ibid., 77-78.

17. Ibid., 78.

18. Watlington, *Partisan Spirit,* 89-98.

19. Marshall, *History of Kentucky,* 230-35; George Morgan Chinn,

Kentucky: Settlement and Statehood, 1750-1800 (Frankfort, 1975), 436-38: Watlington, *Partisan Spirit*, 101-2; Caleb Wallace to James Madison, Sept. 25, 1785, in William T. Hutchinson and William E. Rachal, eds. *The Papers of James Madison*, 24 vols. to date (Chicago, 1962-), 8:369-70; "Letter from Danville," *Maryland Gazette*, May 31, 1785, Draper Collection, 3 JJ 138-39; John Mason Brown, *The Political Beginnings of Kentucky* (Louisville, 1889), 64-68.

20. Clay, "Awful Path to Statehood," 19-20; William Littell, *Political Transactions in and Concerning Kentucky from the First Settlement Thereof, until It became an Independent State in June, 1792* (Frankfort, 1806), 13-14, 63-65; Cotterill, *Pioneer Kentucky*, 211-12.

21. Wallace to Madison, July 12, 1785, *Papers of James Madison*, 8:320-23. See also William H. Whitsitt, *Life and Times of Judge Caleb Wallace* (Louisville, 1888), 114-15.

22. Littell, *Political Transactions*, 67; Watlington, *Partisan Spirit*, 103-4; Hambleton Tapp, *A Sesqui-Centennial History of Kentucky*, 4 vols. (Louisville, 1945), 1:160-61; Marshall, *History of Kentucky*, 1:207-20. The members of the convention are listed in Collins, *History of Kentucky*, 1:354.

23. Marshall, *History of Kentucky*, 1:165. The standard biographies of Wilkinson are: Thomas R. Hay and M.R. Werner, *The Admirable Trumpeter: General James Wilkinson* (Garden City, N.Y., 1941); James R. Jacobs, *Tarnished Warrior* (New York, 1938); and Royal Orman Shreve, *The Finished Scoundrel* (Indianapolis, 1933). James Wilkinson, *Memoirs of My Own Times*, 3 vols. (Philadelphia, 1816), attempts to justify his actions.

24. Marshall, *History of Kentucky*, 1:202-6.

25. Ibid., 247-50.

26. Sept. 25, 1785, *Papers of James Madison*, 8:369.

27. Monroe to Jefferson, Aug. 25, 1785, Julian Boyd and others, eds., *The Papers of Thomas Jefferson*, 23 vols. to date (Princeton, N.J., 1950-), 8:441-42; McDowell to William Fleming, Nov. 11, 1785, Draper Collection, 2 U 139.

28. Marshall, *History of Kentucky*, 260-65; William W. Hening, ed., *Statutes at Large: Being a Collection of All the Laws of Virginia, 1619-1792*, 13 vols. (Richmond, 1809-23), 12:37-40.

29. Madison to Muter, Jan. 7, 1787, "Reminiscences of Kentucky and Her Early Patriots," *Tyler's Quarterly Historical and Genealogical Magazine* 1 (July 1919): 29-30.

30. Watlington, *Partisan Spirit*, 106-13.

31. John Wilson Townsend, *Kentucky in American Letters*,

1784-1912, 2 vols. (Cedar Rapids, Iowa, 1913), 1:26-28; Bodley, *History of Kentucky*, 1:366-67; Marshall, *History of Kentucky*, 1:242-43; Thomas Marshall Green, *The Spanish Conspiracy* (Cincinnati, 1891), 63-65.

32. Kerr, ed., *History of Kentucky*, 1:237-38; Littell, *Political Transactions*, 15-16; Chinn, *Settlement and Statehood*, 444-46; Marshall, *History of Kentucky*, 1:244-52. No list of the members of the Fourth Convention is known to exist. Chinn listed the members of the Fifth Convention as being in the Fourth.

33. Thomas Speed, *The Political Club* (Louisville, 1894), is the most complete account of this interesting organization, but see also Ann Price Combs, "Notes on the Political Club of Danville and Its Members," *FCHQ* 35 (Oct. 1961): 333-52. The Filson Club has the records on which Speed based his book. Speed cited an incorrect date for the visit of Major Beatty. James J. Holmberg, curator of manuscripts, to author, March 20, 1990.

34. Littell, *Political Transactions*, 16-17; Watlington, *Partisan Spirit*, 119; John Marshall (?) to Thomas Marshall, Jan. 11, 1787, *Papers of John Marshall*, 1:201.

35. Hening, *Statutes at Large*, 23:240-42.

36. Madison to Muter, Jan. 7, 1787, Muter, "Reminiscences of Kentucky," 29-30.

37. Madison to Jefferson, Aug. 12, 1786, *Papers of Thomas Jefferson*, 10:233; Watlington, *Partisan Spirit*, 120-22.

38. Collins, *History of Kentucky*, 1:264; Littell, *Political Transactions*, 17-18; Watlington, *Partisan Spirit*, 122-24; James William Hagy, "Arthur Campbell and the Origins of Kentucky: A Reassessment," *FCHQ* 55 (Oct. 1981): 344-74.

3. A Spanish Conspiracy?

1. William Leavy, "A Memoir of Lexington and Its Vicinity," *Register* 41 (July 1943): 259. This "Memoir" was continued in eight issues of the journal, 1942-44.

2. Charles Gayarre, *History of Louisiana*, 4 vols. (4th ed., New Orleans, 1903), 3:194-95; Hay and Werner, *Admirable Trumpeter*, 82-83; François-Xavier Martin, *History of Louisiana*, 2 vols. (New Orleans, 1827-29), 2:92-94.

3. Gayarre, *Louisiana*, 3:195, 199: Hay and Werner, *Admirable Trumpeter*, 86-87; James, *George Rogers Clark*, 376-79; Temple Bodley, ed., *Littell's Political Transactions in and Concerning Kentucky and Letter of George Nicholas, also General Wilkinson's Memorial* (Louis-

ville, 1926), xiii; Watlington, *Partisan Spirit*, 141-42; Bodley, *George Rogers Clark*, 315-22.

4. Hay and Werner, *Admirable Trumpeter*, 88-90; Jacobs, *Tarnished Warrior*, 84; Stevenson interview, Draper Collection, 11 CC 250; Thomas Robson Hay, ed., "Letters of Mrs. Ann Biddle Wilkinson from Kentucky, 1788-1789," *Pennsylvania Magazine of History and Biography* 56 (Jan. 1932): 40; dispatch 13, Sept. 25, 1787, Miro and Intendant Martin Navarro to Antonio Valdes, Pontalba Papers, Bodley Collection, Filson Club, 14.

5. Wilkinson, *Memoirs*, 2:113.

6. Wilkinson to Miro, May 15, 1788, Feb. 12, 1789, Gayarre, *Louisiana*, 3:208-12, 223-40; Watlington, *Partisan Spirit*, 142-45; dispatch of Miro, June 15, 1788, Gayarre, *Louisiana*, 3:212.

7. Watlington, *Partisan Spirit*, 145-47; John Bach McMaster, *History of the People of the United States*, 8 vols. (New York, 1883-1913), 1:521-22; Frederic Austin Ogg, *The Opening of the Mississippi* (New York, 1904), 443; Whitaker, *Spanish-American Frontier*, 97.

8. Depositions of Thomas Barbee and Richard Thomas, in *Innes v Marshall*, 43-44, 109, Durrett Collection; Marshall, *History of Kentucky*, 1:283-84.

9. Gayarre, *Louisiana*, 3:212-13.

10. Daniel A. Yanchisin, "John Bradford, Public Servant," *Register* 68 (Jan. 1970): 60-69; J. Winston Coleman, Jr., "John Bradford and the Kentucky Gazette," *FCHQ* 34 (Jan. 1960): 24-34; Charles R. Staples, *History of Pioneer Lexington* (Lexington, 1939), 39-41. "Kentucke" became "Kentucky" in the issue of March 7, 1788.

11. See especially "A Virginian" in the issues of Aug. 18 and Sept. 1 and "A Kentuckian" in the issue of Sept. 15, 1787.

12. Collins, *History of Kentucky*, 1:354; Green, *Spanish Conspiracy*, 118; Watlington, *Partisan Spirit*, 129-30; Marshall, *History of Kentucky*, 313-15; Thomas Perkins Abernethy, *Western Lands and the American Revolution* (New York, 1959), 326-27; *Maryland Journal*, March 14, 1788, in Draper Collection, 3 JJ 364; Samuel McDowell to Arthur Campbell, Sept. 23, 1787, Draper Collection, 9 DD 46; *Kentucky Gazette*, March 8, 1788.

13. Stuart Seely Sprague, "Senator John Brown of Kentucky, 1757-1837: A Political Biography" (Ph.D. diss., New York Univ., 1972), 15-70; Gayarre, *Louisiana*, 3:241.

14. Brown to James Breckinridge, Jan. 28, 1788, James Breckinridge Papers, Univ. of Virginia; Innes to Brown, Feb. 20, 1788, Innes Papers, Library of Congress.

15. Innes, McDowell, others, to the Court of Fayette County, Feb. 29, 1788, Draper Collection, 11 J 182; Watlington, *Partisan Spirit*, 147-50; unidentified, undated newspaper clipping, "To the Court of Mercer County," Innes Papers, Folder 11.

16. *Kentucky Gazette*, Feb. 23-May 10, 1788; Watlington, *Partisan Spirit*, 151-55.

17. Charles Gano Talbert, "Kentuckians in the Virginia Convention of 1788," *Register* 58 (July 1960): 187-93.

18. Innes to Brown, Feb. 20, 1788, Innes Papers, General Correspondence; Madison to Jefferson, April 22, 1788, *Papers of Thomas Jefferson*, 13:98-99; Madison to Washington, June 4, 13, 1788, *Papers of James Madison*, 11:77, 134; James Breckinridge to John Breckinridge, June 13, 1788, Breckinridge Papers; John Brown to Matthew Walton, June 5, 1788, John Brown Papers, Filson Club; *Debates and Other Proceedings of the Convention of Virginia Convened at Richmond, on Monday the Second Day of June, 1788, for the Purpose of Deliberating on the Constitution Recommended by the Grand Federal Convention* (Richmond, 1805), passim.

19. Talbert, "Kentuckians in the Virginia Convention," 192-93.

20. John Brown to James Breckinridge, March 17, 1788, James Breckinridge Papers; Brown, *Political Beginnings*, 144-45; Sprague, "John Brown," 91-95; Marshall, *History of Kentucky*, 330-50; Watlington, *Partisan Spirit*, 159-64.

21. Sixth Convention Journal, Kentucky Historical Society, 1-2; Watlington, *Partisan Spirit*, 164-65.

22. Sixth Convention Journal, 2; Marshall, *History of Kentucky*, 1:289; Watlington, *Partisan Spirit*, 165-68.

23. Sixth Convention Journal, 3-4; Marshall, *History of Kentucky*, 1:289-90; deposition of Jack Allin, *Innes v Marshall*, 186, Durrett Collection; Watlington, *Partisan Spirit*, 165-69.

24. Sixth Convention Journal, 4-5; Julius F. Prufer, "The Franchise in Virginia from Jefferson through the Convention of 1829," *William and Mary Quarterly*, 2nd ser., 7 (Oct. 1927): 256-57.

25. Marshall, *History of Kentucky*, 1:292-95.

26. Brown, *Political Beginnings*, 155; Abernethy, *Western Lands*, 348; *Kentucky Gazette*, Oct. 15, 1788; Muter in *Western World*, Sept. 6, 1806, reprinted from *The Palladium*, n.d.

27. May 13, 1788, Pontalba Papers.

28. Green, *Spanish Conspiracy*, 211-16; Watlington, *Partisan Spirit*, 174-75.

29. Seventh Convention Journal, Kentucky Historical Society,

1-3; Green, *Spanish Conspiracy*, 221-23; Marshall, *History of Kentucky*, 1:316-18; Clay, "Awful Path," 81-83.

30. Stuart Seely Sprague, "Kentucky Politics and the Heritage of the American Revolution: The Early Years, 1783-1788," *Register* 78 (Spring 1980): 113; *Report of the Select Committee to Whom Was Referred the Information Communicated to the House of Representatives Charging Benjamin Sebastian One of the Judges of the Court of Appeals with Having Received a Pension from the Spanish Government* (Frankfort, 1806), 20-22.

31. Sprague, "Kentucky Politics," 113; Marshall, *History of Kentucky*, 359-62.

32. Seventh Convention Journal, 4-6; Clay, "Awful Path," 86-87; Green, *Spanish Conspiracy*, 221-22.

33. Seventh Convention Journal, 6-7. Green, *Spanish Conspiracy*, 234-35, attributes this delaying resolution to John Brown; the Journal indicates that it was Wilkinson who introduced it.

34. Seventh Convention Journal, 7-14; Green, *Spanish Conspiracy*, 235-37; Watlington, *Partisan Spirit*, 178-79; Joseph Crockett deposition, *Innes v Marshall*, 178, Durrett Collection. Green said John Caldwell of Mercer County collected the signatures. The address to Congress and the address to the General Assembly are given in Marshall, *History of Kentucky*, 1:332-37.

35. Seventh Convention Journal, 11-14; Marshall, *History of Kentucky*, 1:337.

36. Christian, "Wilkinson and Separation," 182-84; Watlington, *Partisan Spirit*, 179-81.

37. Petition of Jan. 15, 1789, Gardoqui Papers, Durett Collection, 5:59-66; Elizabeth Warren, "Benjamin Sebastian and the Spanish Conspiracy in Kentucky," *FCHQ* 20 (April 1946): 112-13; Caruso, *Appalachian Frontier*, 331-33.

38. James A. Padgett, ed., "The Letters of Honorable John Brown to the Presidents of the United States," *Register* 35 (Jan. 1937): 14.

4. The Later Conventions

1. Hening, *Statutes*, 12:788-91.

2. *Kentucky Gazette*, April 25, 1789.

3. Madison to Jefferson, March 29, 1789, *Papers of James Madison*, 12:39.

4. Nicholas to Madison, May 8, 1789, ibid., 138-41; Hugh B. Grigsby, *History of the Virginia Federal Convention of 1788*, 2 vols.

(Richmond, 1890-91), 2:284-96; sketch of Nicholas's life, George Nicholas Papers, Box 1, Folder 1, Durrett Collection; Huntley Dupre, "The Political Ideas of George Nicholas," *Register* 39 (July 1941): 201-5.

5. Washington to Innes, March 2, 1789, *The Writings of George Washington*, ed. John C. Fitzpatrick, 39 vols. (Washington, D.C., 1931-44), 30:214-15; Washington to Marshall, March 27, 1789, ibid., 252-53; James Brown to John Preston, Sept. 3, 1789, Draper Collection, 5 QQ 122.

6. Watlington, *Partisan Spirit*, 184-85; Eighth Convention Journal, Kentucky Historical Society, 1-5, note on back of p. 6.

7. Eighth Convention Journal, 9-11. Pages 12-16 are missing from the Journal.

8. Eighth Convention Journal, 9-11; Marshall, *History of Kentucky*, 394-96.

9. Sprague, "John Brown," 113-14; Talbert, *Logan*, 237-39; Randolph to county lieutenants, June 1, 1789, Littell, *Political Transactions*, 110; Thompson to Madison, June 1, 1790, *Papers of James Madison* 13:236-37; Christian, "Wilkinson and Separation," 244; Nathaniel Richardson to John Breckinridge, Feb. 11, 1790, Breckinridge Papers.

10. Watlington, *Partisan Spirit*, 185-86; Petition No. 58, Robertson, ed., *Kentucky Petitions*, 121-22.

11. Hening, *Statutes*, 13:17-21.

12. Nicholas to Madison, Nov. 2, 1789, *Papers of James Madison* 12:443-45; Nicholas to Madison, Dec. 31, 1790, ibid., 13:337-40.

13. Wilkinson to Miro, Feb. 12, 1789, Christian, "Wilkinson and Separation," 202-7; Gayarre, *Louisiana*, 3:223-40; Wilkinson to Isaac Shelby, Dec. 19, 1789, James Wilkinson transcriptions, Durrett Collection.

14. Christian, "Wilkinson and Separation," 214-19; Hay and Werner, *Admirable Trumpeter*, 95-98; Miro to Antonio Valdes, Head of Colonial Office, Dec. 31, 1789, Pontalba Papers; Wilkinson to Miro, Sept. 17, 1789, ibid.

15. Christian, "Wilkinson and Separation," 222-24; Clay, "Awful Path," 89-92; Wilkinson to Miro, Sept. 17, 1789, Pontalba Papers.

16. Daniel Clark, *Proofs of the Corruption of Gen. James Wilkinson and of His Connection with Aaron Burr. . . .* (Philadelphia, 1809), 9-16; Hay and Werner, *Admirable Trumpeter*, 102-5; Jacobs, *Tarnished Warrior*, 95-105; Christian, "Wilkinson and Separation," 221, 225-26; Ray Allen Billington, *Westward Expansion* (3rd ed., New York, 1967), 233.

17. Hay and Werner, *Admirable Trumpeter*, 102.

18. Wilkinson to "Dear Sir," Jan. 20, 1790, Wilkinson transcriptions, Durrett Collection; Caruso, *Appalachian Frontier*, 334-38. Wilkinson promised to pay an unidentified creditor in full by March 20, 1792. Wilkinson did start receiving a Spanish pension in 1792 when he was a brigadier-general in the American army. Indeed, he got more from Spain after leaving Kentucky than he did during the convention years.

19. Ninth Convention Journal, Kentucky Historical Society, 1-2.

20. Ibid., 3-4. A limited account of this convention is in Marshall, *History of Kentucky*, 393-96.

21. Ninth Convention Journal, 5-8. The Third, Fifth, Seventh, and Eighth conventions had petitioned for separation and statehood; the other conventions had only called for holding additional conventions. On Wednesday John Rogers replaced Lewis as sergeant-at-arms.

22. Ibid., 8-10.

23. Ibid., 11-17.

24. Marshall, *History of Kentucky*, 406-7; Doolan, "Constitutions and Constitutional Conventions," 142; James D. Richardson, comp., *Messages and Papers of the Presidents, 1789-1897*, 10 vols. (Washington, D.C., 1896-99), 1:81-86; Kerr, ed., *History of Kentucky*, 1:254, quotes the jingle.

25. Purvis, "Ethnic Descent of Kentucky's Early Population," 258-61; Tachau, *Federal Courts*, 14; Thompson to Madison, June 1, 1790, *Papers of James Madison*, 13:235-37; Nicholas to John Brown, Dec. 31, 1790, George Nicholas Papers, Kentucky Historical Society; *Return of the Whole Numbers of Persons within the Several Districts of the United States* (Philadelphia, 1791), 51.

26. *Kentucky Gazette*, 1790, passim.; Allen J. Share, *Cities in the Commonwealth* (Lexington, 1982), 9-16; Coward, *Kentucky Constitutions*, 12.

5. WRITING THE CONSTITUTION

1. Coward, *Kentucky Constitutions*, 1-11, is an excellent discussion of this aspect of the background of the convention.

2. Brown to Innes, April 13, 1792, Innes Papers, Library of Congress, General Correspondence, 1792; Taylor to Madison, May 8, 1792, *Papers of James Madison* 14:305.

3. George Muter to Madison, Jan. 6, 1785, *Papers of James Madison* 8:218-19; Caleb Wallace to Madison, July 12, 1785, ibid., 320-24; Madison to Wallace, Aug. 23, 1785, ibid., 350-58; John Brown to

Madison, May 12, 1788, ibid., 11:42-43; Madison to Brown, Oct. 12, 1788, ibid., 280-95; Coward, *Kentucky Constitutions*, 11. In October 1788 Madison sent Brown his detailed "Observations on Jefferson's Draft of a Constitution for Virginia." A copy was later given to George Nicholas.

4. Speed, *Political Club*, 114, 118-19, 125, 130, 139, 144-50, 161-63, 165; Combs, "Political Club," 336-48. Tachau, *Federal Courts*, 40-41 and notes, agrees that the role of Nicholas has been exaggerated and the role of the Political Club has been somewhat neglected.

5. Nicholas to Marshall, May 4, 1789, Innes Papers, Library of Congress, General Correspondence, 1789; Nicholas to Madison, June 20, 1791, *Papers of James Madison*, 14:33; Dupre, "Political Ideas of Nicholas," 201-23.

6. Watlington, *Partisan Spirit*, 213-17; *Kentucky Gazette*, Oct. 1, 15, 1791.

7. *Kentucky Gazette*, Oct. 22, 1791.

8. Ibid., Feb. 11, 1792.

9. Innes to Thomas Jefferson, Aug. 27, 1791, *Jefferson Papers*, 22:86; "A.B.C.," *Kentucky Gazette*, Sept. 24, 1791; "Will Wisp," ibid., Oct. 15, 1791; "Felte Firebrand," ibid., Nov. 12, 1791; "A Medlar," ibid., Nov. 19, 1791; "H.S.B.M.," ibid., Nov. 19, 26, 1791, Jan. 7, 1792; "Salamander," ibid., Dec. 24, 1791.

10. "Philip Philips," *Kentucky Gazette*, Nov. 26, Dec. 3, 1791; "H.S.B.M.," ibid., Feb. 25, 1789; "Little Brutus," ibid., Dec. 10, 17, 24, 1791; "Brutus Senior," ibid., March 10, 1792; "A.B.C.," ibid., Dec. 3, 10, 1791; "A Citizen," ibid., Dec. 17, 1791; "X.Y.Z.," ibid., Feb. 18, 1792.

11. Watlington, *Partisan Spirit*, 212; "The Disinterested Citizen," Dec. 11, 1790, March 5, 12, July 2, Oct. 22, 29, Dec. 31, 1791, Feb. 11, 25, 1792. The quotations are from the issue of Feb. 11, 1792.

12. Coward, *Kentucky Constitutions*, 20-22; Watlington, *Partisan Spirit*, 216-18; Clay, "Awful Path," 114-21; H. Marshall, *History of Kentucky*, 1:394.

13. Tenth Convention Journal, Kentucky Historical Society, 1-2; Coward, *Kentucky Constitutions*, 25.

14. Tenth Convention Journal, 3.

15. Ibid., 3-5; Clay, "Awful Path," 123-28.

16. Tenth Convention Journal, 5-7; Clay, "Awful Path," 129-31; Watlington, *Partisan Spirit*, 218; H. Marshall, *History of Kentucky*, 1:395-96.

17. Tenth Convention Journal, 7-8; Vernon P. Martin, "Father Rice, the Preacher Who Followed the Frontier," *FCHQ* 29 (Dec. 1955),

324-30; David Rice, *Slavery Inconsistent with Justice and Good Policy, Proved by a Speech Delivered in the Convention, Held at Danville, Kentucky* (Philadelphia, 1792), passim.; Coward, *Kentucky Constitutions,* 36-41; Lowell H. Harrison, *The Antislavery Movement in Kentucky* (Lexington, 1978), 18-24.

18. Tenth Convention Journal, 7-8, 22; Clay, "Awful Path," 133-37; Coward, *Kentucky Constitutions,* 41-45; Doolan, "Constitutions and Conventions," 140-41; Taylor to Madison, April 16, 1792, *Papers of James Madison,* 14:289. Three Jefferson County delegates, Breckinridge, Bullitt, and R. Taylor, did not vote.

19. Tenth Convention Journal, 9-19; Nicholas notes on the resolutions, Nicholas Papers, Durrett Collection, Box 1, Folder 13.

20. Tenth Convention Journal, 19-20; Clay, "Awful Path," 140-41; Richard H. Caldemeyer, "The Career of George Nicholas" (Ph.D. diss., Indiana Univ., 1951), 74-75.

21. Tenth Convention Journal, 20.

22. Ibid.; McDowell to Andrew Reid, April 18, 1792, Samuel McDowell Papers, Filson Club.

23. Tenth Convention Journal, 21-23; Clay, "Awful Path," 142-44. The constitution is on pages 23-47 of the Journal.

24. Tenth Convention Journal, 47-48.

25. Governor Isaac Shelby, Enrolled Bills, Book, 2, June 28, 1792, Kentucky State Archives, Frankfort.

6. The Constitution Achieved

1. George L. Willis, *Kentucky Constitutions and Constitutional Conventions* (Frankfort, 1930), 53; Bennett H. Young, *History and Texts of the Three Constitutions of Kentucky* (Louisville, 1890), 52, 73-74.

2. John D. Barnhart, "Frontiersmen and Planters in the Formation of Kentucky," *Journal of Southern History* 7 (Feb. 1941): 33-35, especially note on 34. His summary used a detailed comparison made by Clara Campbell Holmes, "The First Kentucky Constitution" (MA thesis, Louisiana State Univ., 1940), 40, 93-115, 93a-115a.

3. For an account of the calling of the 1799 convention see Lowell H. Harrison, *John Breckinridge, Jeffersonian Republican* (Louisville, 1969), 93-109. Alexander S. Bullitt presided in 1799 and Thomas Todd was the clerk.

4. Article I, Sections 1-6, 26.

5. Article I, Sections 7-15.

6. Article I, Sections 16-23, 27-29.

7. Coward, *Kentucky Constitutions*, 28-29.

8. Ibid, 29-31; Article II, Sections 1-8, 15-17.

9. Article II, Sections 9-14.

10. Article III, Sections 1-3; Coward, *Kentucky Constitutions*, 32-33, 76; Nicholas to Madison, May 2, 1792, *Papers of James Madison*, 14:296-98.

11. Article IV, Sections 1-3.

12. Article V, Sections 1-2, 6-7; Coward, *Kentucky Constitutions*, 33-35.

13. Article V, Sections 3-5.

14. Article VI.

15. Article VII; Article VIII, Section 5.

16. Article VIII, Sections 1-7.

17. Nicholas to Madison, May 2, 1792, *Papers of James Madison*, 14:297.

18. Article IX.

19. Article X.

20. Madison to Caleb Wallace, Aug. 23, 1785, *Papers of James Madison*, 8:355-56; Article XI; Coward, *Kentucky Constitutions*, 45-46. An excellent account of the second convention is in Coward, *Kentucky Constitutions*, 97-161.

21. Article XII, Sections 1-28.

22. Schedule, Sections 1-11.

23. Otis K. Rice, *Frontier Kentucky* (Lexington, 1975), 114-16; Tapp, *History of Kentucky*, 2:565-68. A good brief history of Kentucky's public schools is Ellis Hartford, *The Little White Schoolhouse* (Lexington, 1977).

24. *Kentucky Gazette*, Jan. 14, 1792.

25. Thomas D. Clark, "Kentucky Education Through Two Centuries of Political and Social Change," *Register* 83 (Summer 1985): 176-77.

26. Nicholas to Madison, May 2, 1792, *Papers of James Madison*, 14:296.

7. IMPLEMENTING THE CONSTITUTION

1. *Kentucky Gazette*, May 5, 12, 19, 1792.

2. *House Journal*, June 8, 1792 (the House and Senate journals for the first session of the General Assembly were published and bound together [Lexington: John Bradford, 1793]); *Kentucky Gazette*, May 19, 1792.

3. Paul W. Beasley, "Isaac Shelby," in Harrison, ed., *Kentucky's Governors*, 1-6; Sylvia Wrobel and George Grider, *Isaac Shelby: Kentucky's First Governor and Hero of Three Wars* (Danville, 1974), 4-67; Orlando Brown, "The Governors of Kentucky, 1792-1824," *Register* 49 (Jan. 1951), 24-26, 93-96; Isaac Shelby, "Autobiography," Durrett Collection.

4. *Kentucky Gazette*, June 9, 1792; Charles R. Staples, "Kentucky's First Inauguration Day," *Register* 31 (April 1933), 146-51; Wrobel and Grider, *Shelby*, 85-87; George W. Ranck, *History of Lexington, Kentucky* (Cincinnati, 1872), 171-72.

5. Federal Writers Project, *Lexington and the Bluegrass Country* (Lexington, 1938), 12; *Senate Journal*, June 4-6, 1792; *House Journal*, June 4-6, 1792.

6. Watlington, *Partisan Spirit*, 59-60; *Senate Journal*, June 6-7, 1792.

7. *Senate Journal*, June 7, 14, 25, 28. Some of the most important records of Shelby's first administration are: Official Papers, 1791-1796; Enrolled Bills; Memorandum Book, 1792-1794; and Executive Journal (all in Kentucky State Archives). See Mabel Weaks, ed., "Memorandum Book of Governor Isaac Shelby, 1792-1794," *FCHQ* 30 (July 1956): 203-31; "Excerpts from the Executive Journal of Gov. Isaac Shelby," *Register* 27 (Sept. 1929): 587-94, and 28 (Jan., April, July 1930), 1-24, 139-50, 203-13; Isaac Shelby Papers, 1777-1844, Filson Club.

8. *House Journal*, June 28, 1792; *Senate Journal*, June 28, 1792.

9. Durrett, *Centenary of Kentucky*, 72.

10. *House and Senate Journals*, passim.

11. *House Journal*, June 5 -7, 19, 27, 29, 1792; *Senate Journal*, June 25-29, 1792.

12. *House Journal*, June 7, 21, 1792; Act 6, Establishing a permanent revenue, and Act 30, Covering fees for certain offices, *Acts of First Session of General Assembly, 1792* (Lexington, 1792). Both Butler, *History of the Commonwealth*, 213-14, and Marshall, *History of Kentucky*, 2:17, agree upon the pound-dollar ratio in 1792.

13. Act 35, Establishing county courts, courts of quarterly sessions, and Court of Oyer and Terminer; Act 36, Establishing the Court of Appeals, *Acts of First Session*; *Senate Journal*, June 13, 1792; Marshall, *History of Kentucky*, 2:24, 27; Ireland, *County Courts*, 2-18; William C. Richardson, *An Administrative History of Kentucky Courts to 1850* (Frankfort, 1983), 2-6.

14. *Senate Journal*, June 26, 1792.

15. The Woodford Courthouse Act, dated June 26, 1792, is not numbered but is inserted between Acts 5 and 6 signed on the same day. No Act 8 is listed by that number, so its insertion was probably intended to take care of the numbering problem.

16. *House Journal*, June 18, 1792; *Senate Journal*, June 18, 25, 1792.

17. *House Journal*, June 18, 20, 1792; Bayless E. Hardin, "The Capitols of Kentucky," *Register* 43 (July 1945): 175-79; Marshall, *History of Kentucky*, 2:5-6; Andrew Holmes to Harry Innes, April 8, 1792, Innes Papers, General Correspondence, 1792; J.T. Dorris, "A 1792 Offer for the Location of the Capital of Kentucky at Boonesboro," *Register* 31 (April 1933): 174-75.

Bibliographical Note

A great mass of primary and secondary sources exists for the pioneer and formative periods of Kentucky's history, but much of it was of little use for this study. Kentuckians of that era who left written records were much more concerned with Indian raids and land deals than with the political developments that ultimately led to statehood. Pertinent sources were fragmented and widely scattered. This "Note" is confined largely to the more important materials and those a reader might find most easily. The endnotes indicate a number of additional sources, but they represent only a fraction of the ones examined in the preparation of this work.

The primary information for this study should be in the journals of the ten conventions, but several of them have disappeared, and none of them includes any of the debates or discussions. The journals of the last five conventions went to the University of Chicago when the Reuben T. Durrett Collection was purchased, but Kentucky State Librarian Mrs. Emma Guy Cromwell was able to recover them. They are now in the Manuscripts Division, Kentucky Historical Society. Pages 12-16 of the Eighth Convention journal are blank. The First Convention Journal has been published: Thomas P. Abernethy, "Journal of the First Kentucky Convention, December 27, 1784-January 5, 1785," *Journal of Southern History* 1 (Feb. 1935): 67-78. The journal of the first constitutional convention was published as a part of the sesquicentennial celebration of statehood; *Journal of the First Constitutional Convention of Kentucky, Held in Danville, Kentucky, April 2 to 19, 1792* (Lexington, 1942). Although all of the conventions were apparently open to the public, the *Kentucky Gazette* made no effort to cover the sessions and published only occasional excerpts from the journals.

Several sets of government records were useful for this period. The *Calendar of Virginia State Papers and Other Manuscripts,* 11 vols. (Richmond, 1875-93), has a great deal of pertinent correspondence, and James R. Robertson, *Petitions of the Early Inhabitants of Kentucky* (Louisville, 1914), details many of the Kentucky complaints. Virginia laws are found in William W. Hening, comp., *Statutes at Large: Being a Collection of All the Laws of Virginia, 1619-1792,* 13 vols. (Richmond, 1809-23). W.C. Ford and others, eds., *Journals of the Continental Congress, 1774-1789,* 34 vols. (Washington, 1904-37), and *Debates and Proceedings in the Congress of the United States, 1789-1824,* 42 vols. (Washington, 1834-56), have the national legislative reactions to Kentucky's search for statehood. The executive responses are in James D. Richardson, ed., *Messages and Papers of the Presidents,* 10 vols. (Washington, 1896-99). Kentucky's first constitution is printed and discussed in Bennett H. Young, *History and Texts of the Three Constitutions of Kentucky* (Louisville, 1890), and George L. Willis, *Kentucky Constitutions and Constitutional Conventions, 1784-1932* (Frankfort, 1930). The Kentucky Historical Society has the House and Senate journals for the first session of the General Assembly in June 1792; the Kentucky Library, Western Kentucky University, has both a microfilm and a typescript copy. The legislative results of the first General Assembly are in *Acts of First Session of General Assembly, 1792* (Lexington, 1792); the changes made by subsequent legislatures are in William Littell, comp., *Statute Law of Kentucky,* 5 vols. (Frankfort, 1809-19). Governor Shelby's official papers for his first administration deal largely with routine matters; they seldom reflect his thinking on issues and personalities. Among the most useful are: Official Papers, 1792-1796; Enrolled Bills Books; Executive Journal; and Memorandum Book, 1792-1794, all in the Kentucky State Archives. Some of these records have been published, at least in part. See especially: "Excerpts from Executive Journal of Gov. Isaac Shelby," *Register* 27 (Sept. 1929): 587-94, 28 (Jan., April, July 1930): 1-24, 139-50, 203-13; and Mabel C. Weaks, ed., "Memorandum Book of Governor Isaac Shelby, 1792-1794," *FCHQ* 30 (July 1956): 203-31.

The convention journals can be augmented to a limited degree by contemporary correspondence, but no Kentuckian is known to have left a sizable body of information about the political road to statehood. Most helpful was William T. Hutchinson and William M.E. Rachal, eds., *The Papers of James Madison,* 24 vols. to date (Chicago, 1962-). Several Kentuckians frequently sought Madison's advice, and he was generous in his responses. Of less use were: Julian P. Boyd and others, eds., *The Papers of Thomas Jefferson*, 23 vols. to date (Princeton, N.J., 1950-); John C. Fitzpatrick, ed., *The Writings of George Washington*, 39 vols. (Washington, D.C., 1931-44); and Herbert A. Johnson, ed., *The Papers of John Marshall*, 5 vols. to date (Chapel Hill, 1974-). The Draper Collection (Wisconsin Historical Society; microfilm at Western Kentucky University) contains a number of scattered letters, interviews, and clippings. The Durrett Collection (Special Collections, University of Chicago) was most helpful with the Isaac Shelby Papers, the George Nicholas Papers, the Gardoqui Papers, the depositions in the *Innes* v *Marshall* case, and the James Wilkinson Papers scattered throughout the collection. A great amount of information concerning Wilkinson and the Spanish Conspiracy is in the Pontalba Papers, the Bodley Collection, at The Filson Club. These papers consist of translated typescripts of papers from the Spanish archives in the possession of the Louisiana Historical Society. Other useful collections at The Filson Club include the John Brown Papers, the Isaac Shelby Papers, and the Samuel McDowell Papers. Most of the latter were published in Otto A. Rothert, ed., "Thirteen Letters by Samuel McDowell," *FCHQ* 16 (July 1942): 172-86. The Kentucky Historical Society has small holdings of papers for John Brown, George Nicholas, Harry Innes, Isaac Shelby, and James Wilkinson, in addition to the official papers mentioned above. Among the most helpful collections in the Manuscript Division, Library of Congress, are the Breckinridge Family Papers, the James Brown Papers, the Harry Innes Papers, and the Isaac Shelby Papers. The James Madison Papers and the Thomas Jefferson Papers were used in the published editions. Special Collections, Margaret I. King Library, University of Kentucky, has several useful items in the papers of John Bradford, Isaac Shelby, and Hubbard Taylor.

Journals have published a number of letters from this period in Kentucky history. Among the most interesting are: Thomas Robson Hay, ed., "Letters of Mrs. Ann Biddle Wilkinson from Kentucky, 1788-1789," *Pennsylvania Magazine of History and Biography* 56 (Jan. 1931), 33-55; Huntley Dupre, ed., "Three Letters of George Nicholas to John Brown," *Register* 41 (Jan. 1943): 1-10; Richard J. Cox, ed., "'A Touch of Kentucky News & State of Politics': Two Letters of Levi Todd, 1784 and 1788," *Register* 76 (July 1978): 216-22; James A. Padgett, ed., "The Letters of Honorable John Brown to the Presidents of the United States," *Register* 35 (Jan. 1937): 1-28; and Wade Hall, ed., "Along the Wilderness Trail: A Young Lawyer's 1785 Letter from Danville, Kentucky, to Massachusetts," *FCHQ* 61 (July 1987): 283-94.

Virginia Smith Herold, ed., "Joel Watkins' Diary of 1789," *Register* 34 (July 1936): 215-50, is of particular interest because he went to Kentucky down the Ohio River and returned east by the Wilderness Road.

As the endnotes indicate, an invaluable study of this period is Patricia Watlington, *The Partisan Spirit: Kentucky Politics, 1779-1792* (New York, 1972). No one has studied the politics of the period as thoroughly as she has done. Although one may disagree with her on such points as the presence of political parties in Kentucky before the 1790s, her work is based on the most meticulous scholarship. Another fine scholarly work is Joan Wells Coward, *Kentucky in the New Republic: The Process of Constitution Making* (Lexington, 1979). It is especially good on the transition from the constitution of 1792 to the one of 1799. William Wilson Hume Clay, "Kentucky: The Awful Path to Statehood" (Ph.D. diss., Univ. of Kentucky, 1966), and Clara Campbell Holmes, "The First Kentucky Constitution" (MA thesis, Louisiana State Univ., 1940), were also useful. Holmes made a section by section analysis of the origins of the 1792 Kentucky constitution that was used in John D. Barnhart, "Frontiersmen and Planters in the Formation of Kentucky," *Journal of Southern History* 7 (Feb. 1941): 19-36.

Some of the early histories of Kentucky, although usually very biased, contain information on this period not found elsewhere. Humphrey Marshall, who became a leading state Federalist, did not publish the projected second volume of *The History of Kentucky* (Frankfort, 1812). Instead, a dozen years later he issued an extended and revised book of the same title (Frankfort, 1824) in two volumes. Marshall had access to materials that later disappeared, and his personality sketches of such opponents as James Wilkinson make good reading. William Littell was employed by several of Marshall's foes to prove their innocence; his book led to Marshall's 1812 effort to prove their guilt. Littell, *Political Transactions in and Concerning Kentucky From the First Settlement Thereof, Until It Became an Independent State, in June 1792* (Frankfort, 1806), is best used in Temple Bodley, ed., *Littell's Political Transactions in and Concerning Kentucky and Letter of George Nicholas, Also General Wilkinson's Memorial* (Louisville, 1926). Bodley included considerable material not in the original. Mann Butler, *A History of the Commonwealth of Kentucky* (Louisville, 1834), also defends the men accused of participation in the Spanish Conspiracy. The dispute continued into the late nineteenth century. John Mason Brown, *The Political Beginnings of Kentucky* (Louisville, 1889), is a defense of John Brown and his associates by a grandson who ignored contrary information. In a counterattack,

Brown accused Humphrey Marshall of complicity in a British conspiracy. He was answered by Thomas Marshall Green, *The Spanish Conspiracy* (Cincinnati, 1891), another highly partisan work by a grandson of Humphrey Marshall.

Among later and less biased histories that have considerable information on this period, these are most useful: Lewis and Richard H. Collins, *History of Kentucky*, 2 vols. (Covington, 1874); William Elsey Connelley and E.M. Coulter, *History of Kentucky*, ed. Judge Charles Kerr, 5 vols. (Chicago, 1922); Temple Bodley, *History of Kentucky*, 4 vols. (Louisville, 1928); Hambleton Tapp, *A Sesqui-Centennial History of Kentucky*, 4 vols. (Louisville, 1945); and George Morgan Chinn, *Kentucky: Settlement and Statehood, 1750-1800* (Frankfort, 1975). Two Louisiana histories are especially good on the Spanish Conspiracy and James Wilkinson: Charles Gayarre, *History of Louisiana*, 4 vols. (4th ed., New Orleans, 1903), and François-Xavier Martin, *History of Louisiana*, 2 vols. (New Orleans, 1827-29).

James Wilkinson, *Memoirs of My Own Times*, 3 vols. (Philadelphia, 1816), is disappointing. A self-serving defense of his career, it is less interesting than its author. The standard biographies of Wilkinson, all of which devote considerable attention to his Kentucky years, are: Royal Ornan Shreve, *The Finished Scoundrel* (Indianapolis, 1933); James Ripley Jacobs, *Tarnished Warrior* (New York, 1938); and Thomas Robson Hay and M.R. Werner, *The Admirable Trumpeter* (Garden City, New York, 1941). His role in Kentucky's separation movement is detailed in Percy Willis Christian, "General James Wilkinson and Kentucky Separation, 1784-1798" (Ph.D. diss., Northwestern Univ., 1935). A thoughtful analysis of his career is Thomas R. Hay, "Some Reflections on the Career of General James Wilkinson," *Mississippi Valley Historical Review* 21 (March 1935): 471-94.

Numerous articles have been written about the Spanish Conspiracy. One of the best is W.A. Shepherd, "Wilkinson and the Beginnings of the Spanish Conspiracy," *American Historical Review* 9 (July 1904): 490-506. Shepherd also edited in the same issue "Papers Bearing on James Wilkinson's Relations with Spain, 1787-1789," 748-66. Elizabeth Warren wrote three articles dealing with aspects of the conspiracy: "John Brown and His Influence on Kentucky Politics, 1784-1795," *Register* 36 (Jan. 1938): 61-65; "Benjamin Sebastian and the Spanish Conspiracy of Kentucky," *FCHQ* 20 (April 1946): 107-30; and "Senator John Brown's Role in the Kentucky Spanish Conspiracy," *FCHQ* 36 (April 1962): 159-76. She found Sebastian guilty, Brown innocent. Her verdict on Brown is challenged by Patricia Watlington, "John Brown and the Spanish Conspiracy," *Virginia Magazine of History and Biography* 75 (Jan. 1967): 52-68. Daniel Clark, *Proofs of the Corruption of Gen. James Wilkinson and of His Connection with Aaron Burr . . .* (Philadelphia, 1809), and *Report of the Select Committee to Whom Was Referred the Information Communicated to the House of Representatives Charging Benjamin Sebastian One of the Judges of the Court of Appeals with Having Received a Pension from the Spanish Government* (Frankfort, 1806), contain information about Wilkinson's involvement.

Several biographies and special studies other than the Wilkinson ones discuss the roles of their subjects in the separation movement. The abysmal penmanship of George Nicholas has discouraged a number of would-be biographers. Richard H. Caldemeyer, "The Career of George Nicholas" (Ph.D. diss., Indiana Univ., 1951), did not use many of the Nicholas manuscripts. His study should be supplemented by Huntley Dupre, "The Political Ideas of George Nicholas," *Register* 39 (July 1941): 201-23. One of the best biographies of early Kentucky leaders is Charles Gano Talbert, *Benjamin Logan: Kentucky Frontiersman* (Lexington, 1962). Logan was one of the few pioneers who remained politically active into the statehood era. John Brown is best discussed in Stuart Seely Sprague, "Senator John Brown of Kentucky, 1757-1837: A Political Biography" (Ph.D. diss., New York Univ., 1972). Isaac Shelby merits a full-scale biography; the best to date is Sylvia Wrobel and George Grider, *Isaac Shelby: Kentucky's First Governor and Hero of Three Wars* (Danville, 1974). William H. Whitsitt, *Life and Times of Judge Caleb Wallace* (Louisville, 1888), is not very informative on the separation movement. The aborted role of George Rogers Clark and his association with James Wilkinson are discussed in many places, including: James A. James, *Life of George Rogers Clark* (Chicago, 1928); James A. James, ed., *The George Rogers Clark Papers*, 2 vols. (Springfield, Ill., 1912, 1926); and Temple Bodley, *George Rogers Clark: His Life and Public Services* (Boston, 1926). Daniel A. Yanchisin, "John Bradford, Public Servant," *Register* 68 (Jan. 1970): 60-69, and J. Winston Coleman, Jr., "John Bradford and the Kentucky Gazette," *FCHQ* 34 (Jan. 1960): 24-34, tell of the state's first newspaper editor. A brief history of Father Rice is in Vernon P. Martin, "Father Rice, the Preacher Who Followed the Frontier," *FCHQ* 29 (Oct. 1955), 324-30.

John Anthony Caruso, *The Appalachian Frontier* (Indianapolis, 1959), Thomas Perkins Abernethy, *Western Lands and the American Revolution* (New York, 1959), and John D. Barnhart, *Valley of Democracy: The Frontier versus the Plantation in the Ohio Valley, 1775-1818*

(Bloomington, Ind., 1953), are among the many works that deal generally with the period when Kentucky was a part of the West. Kentucky's involvement in the diplomacy of the period is detailed in Arthur Preston Whitaker, *The Spanish-American Frontier: 1783-1795* (Boston, 1927), and Samuel Flagg Bemis, *Jay's Treaty: A Study in Commerce and Diplomacy* (New York, 1924). The best brief account of Kentucky's pioneer stage is Otis K. Rice, *Frontier Kentucky* (Lexington, 1975), although R.S. Cotterill, *History of Pioneer Kentucky* (Cincinnati, 1917), is still useful. All of the older histories have extensive accounts of that era. Two excellent articles by Neal O. Hammon discuss the vital issue of land ownership: "Land Acquisition on the Kentucky Frontier," *Register* 78 (Autumn 1980): 297-321, and "Settlers, Land Jobbers, and Outlayers: A Quantitative Analysis of Land Acquisition on the Kentucky Frontier," *Register* 84 (Summer 1986): 241-62. Thomas D. Clark, *Agrarian Kentucky* (Lexington, 1977), discusses the early development of agriculture in the state and the importance of the Mississippi River outlet. A different view of the state and its people is Arthur K. Moore, *The Frontier Mind: A Cultural Analysis of the Kentucky Frontiersman* (Lexington, 1957). The composition of the early population is studied in Thomas L. Purvis, "The Ethnic Descent of Kentucky's Early Population: A Statistical Investigation of European and American Sources of Immigration, 1790-1820," *Register* 80 (Summer 1982): 253-66.

The courts had an important role in early Kentucky history; the demand for an adequate system was one of the causes of separation. Samuel M. Wilson, *The First Land Court of Kentucky, 1779-1780* (Lexington, 1923), discusses one of the most important of the early courts. Robert M. Ireland, *The County Courts in Antebellum Kentucky* (Lexington, 1972), and William C. Richardson, *An Administrative History of Kentucky Courts to 1850* (Frankfort, 1983), provide an overview of the system developed in 1792 and afterward. Mary K. Bonsteel Tachau, *Federal Courts in the Early Republic: Kentucky, 1789-1816* (Princeton, 1978), is also the best account of Harry Innes. The overall importance of the too-numerous counties is studied in Robert M. Ireland, *The County in Kentucky History* (Lexington, 1976).

The incomplete records of the Danville Political Club are in The Filson Club. Some of them have been published in Thomas Speed, *The Political Club* (Louisville, 1894), but it should be supplemented by Ann Price Combs, "Notes on the Political Club of Danville and Its Members," *FCHQ* 35 (Oct. 1961): 333-52.

Although early Kentucky was predominantly rural, the small

towns were exceedingly important. Allen J. Share, *Cities in the Commonwealth* (Lexington, 1982), gives a convenient overview but pays little attention to developments before the nineteenth century. Calvin Morgan Fackler, *Early Days in Danville* (Louisville, 1941), has long been the standard history of Danville during the period when it was the political center of Kentucky. Among the general works on Lexington are: George W. Ranck, *History of Lexington, Kentucky* (Cincinnati, 1872); Federal Writers Project, *Lexington and the Bluegrass Country* (Lexington, 1938); Charles R. Staples, *History of Pioneer Lexington* (Lexington, 1959); and John D. Wright, Jr., *Lexington: Heart of the Bluegrass* (Lexington, 1982). The most complete account of pioneer Frankfort is Willard Rouse Jillson, *Early Frankfort and Franklin County, Kentucky . . . 1750-1850* (Louisville, 1936); less comprehensive is Nettie Henry Glenn, *Early Frankfort History* (Frankfort, 1986).

The overland route into Kentucky has often been described. Wm. Allen Pusey, *The Wilderness Road to Kentucky* (New York, 1921), is one of the most detailed accounts, but it should be supplemented by Thomas L. Connelly, "Gateway to Kentucky: The Wilderness Road, 1748-1792," *Register* 59 (April 1961): 109-32, and Neal Owen Hammon, "Early Roads into Kentucky," *Register* 68 (April 1970): 91-131.

Many details of the first inauguration are missing. The most complete account is Charles R. Staples, "Kentucky's First Inauguration Day," *Register* 31 (April 1933): 146-51. A good description of the state's capitols is in Bayless E. Hardin, "The Capitols of Kentucky," *Register* 43 (July 1945): 173-200. J.T. Dorris edited "A 1792 Offer for the Location of the Capital of Kentucky at Boonesboro," *Register* 31 (April 1933): 174-75.

Niels Henry Sonne, *Liberal Kentucky, 1780-1928* (New York, 1933), found some early traces of liberalism in the 1792 constitution and the antislavery movement, as did E. Merton Coulter, "Early Frontier Democracy in the First Kentucky Constitution," *Political Science Quarterly* 39 (Dec. 1924): 665-77. The influence of the recent Revolution is discussed in Stuart Seely Sprague, "Kentucky Politics and the Heritage of the American Revolution: The Early Years, 1783-1788," *Register* 78 (Spring 1980): 98-114.

Voting requirements prior to statehood are covered in Julius Prufer, "The Franchise in Virginia from Jefferson through the Convention of 1829," *William and Mary Quarterly*, 2nd ser., 7 (Oct. 1927): 255-70, and 8 (Jan. 1928): 17-32. Charles Gano Talbert describes the inactive role of the Kentucky delegates in "Kentuckians in the Virginia Convention of 1788," *Register* 58 (July 1960): 187-93, and documentation of that point is supplied by Hugh B. Grigsby, *History of the Virginia Federal Convention of 1788*, 2 vols. (Richmond, 1890-91). A fine survey of the state's attitude toward education, including its neglect in 1792, is Thomas D. Clark, "Kentucky Education through Two Centuries of Political and Social Change," *Register* 83 (Summer 1985): 163-201.

Index

"A.B.C.," 100, 101
Able, Robert, 133
"A Citizen," 101-2
administration: deficient in Kentucky, 15-16
agriculture, 92; increase in 1784, 9; surplus crops, 48-49; advance in prices, 53
Allen, John, 133, 134, 147
Allin, Thomas, 87
"A Medler," 100, 101
amendments: not provided for in 1792, 126
American Revolution in South, 6. See also King's Mountain, battle of; Point Pleasant, battle of
"An Address to the Inhabitants of the District of Kentucky," 32
Anderson, Robert C., 84
antislavery: at Tenth Convention, 108-9
Article IX: slavery in 1792 constitution, 110-11
Articles of Confederation, 3-4, 22, 45, 56, 57; rejects admission of Kentucky, 61-62
attorney general, office of, 120-21

Baily, John, 110
Barbee, Joshua, 78, 104
Barbee, Thomas, 137
Bardstown, 146
Barnett, Joseph, 27
Barnhart, John D.: and origins of 1792 constitution, 116
Beall, Walter, 133
Beatty, Major Erkuries, 44
Bill of Rights, 126-27, 146; federal, 59; and Danville Political Club, 95-96; in 1792 constitution, 127
blacks: denied suffrage, 122. See also antislavery; slavery
Bodley, Temple, 8
Boone, Daniel, 2, 6
Boone, Squire, 26
Boonesborough (Boonesboro): meeting at, 2; Tories at, 6; seeks capital site, 147-48
boundary of Virginia, 3
Bourbon County, 9, 105, 132-33
Bourbon County committee, 98-99, 101
Bowman, Abraham, 132
Bradford, John, 132, 138, 145; founds Kentucky Gazette, 54-55

Breckinridge, James, at 1788 Virginia ratifying convention, 60

Breckinridge, John, 60

Breckinridge, Robert, 23, 55, 61, 133, 146; Speaker of House of Representatives, 138

Breckinridge, William, 15

Brodrick, David, 133

Brooks, Ebenezer, 22, 26, 31, 34; on separation, 20, 55. *See also* partisan faction

Brown, James, 77, 139

Brown, John, 24, 41, 47, 67-68, 72; sent to Congress, 56; described, 56-57; and U.S. constitution, 57, 59, 60; seeks admission of Kentucky, 61-62; talks with Gardoqui, 62; and Sixth Convention, 65; at Seventh Convention, 68-69; on constitutional convention, 94; U.S. senator, 146. *See also* Spanish Conspiracy; Wilkinson, James

"Brutus Senior," 101

Bryan, John, 87

Bullitt, Alexander Scott, 84, 88, 133, 134, 138, 139; and James Wilkinson, 53

Bullitt, Robert, 23

Bullock, Rice, 61

Butler, Mann, 11-12

Caldwell, John, 134

Caldwell, Robert, 84

Campbell, Arthur, 46

Campbell, John, 22

Campbell, William, 132

capital, state: selection process for, 125-26; selected, 146-48

Caruso, John, 14

Cave, William, 133

Cave Run Creek, 54

census, 29, 79; in 1790, 91

Chambers, James, 133

Cherokees, 2, 20, 134

Chickamaugas, 20

Clark, Daniel, 85

Clark, George Rogers: threatens separation, 1; delegate to Virginia, 1-2; opposes Transylvania Company, 3; rejects separation, 12; criticism of, 15; and 1786 Indian campaign, 44; discredited by Wilkinson, 50

Clark, Thomas D., 129

Clarke, Thomas, 132

Clay, Green, 84

Clay, Thomas, 132, 143

Clift, Henry, 133

Clinkenbeard, William, 6

Comes, Mrs. William, 128

commerce, 48-49, 92. *See also* Jay-Gardoqui Treaty; Mississippi River; Wilkinson, James

committee, county: used by partisans, 97-98; in Bourbon County, 98-99, 101

committee, select, in General Assembly, 142

Committee of Correspondence: in Pittsburgh, 46-47

Compact, Virginia. *See* enabling acts: Fourth

Congress, Second Continental, 3, 12

Congress, U.S.: admits Kentucky, 90. *See also* Articles of Confederation

Conn, Noltey, 61

Constitution, federal: opposed by court faction, 57-58; ratified by Virginia, 59-61

Constitution, Kentucky, of 1792: drafted, 104-14; nature of, 115-18, 130; name of state, 117; legislature, 118-20;

electoral college, 118, 120; executive, 119-21; attorney general, 120-21; secretary of state, 120-21; suffrage, 121-22; judiciary, 122-23; sheriffs and coroners, 123; militia, 123-24; court clerks, 124; oath of office, 124; treason defined, 124; finances, 124; Virginia compact, 124; slavery protected, 125; selection of capital, 125-26; calling another convention, 126; bill of rights, 127; transition schedule, 127-28; education ignored, 128; reaction to, 129-30; text in full, 152-68

Convention, Virginia, of 1788: to ratify federal constitution, 59-61

conventions, in Kentucky:
—First: background to, 19-21; members of, 25-26; work of, 26-30; recorded vote, 28; grievances listed, 28-29; call for Second Convention, 29; factions in, 30
—Second: membership questioned, 30-31; separation petition not sent, 31; calls for Third Convention, 31; issues "Address to the Inhabitants," 32
—Third: calls for separation, 34-35; lists grievances, 34-35; issues "To the Inhabitants," 35, 36-37; address to General Assembly, 38
—Fourth: called, 41; elections for, 43-44; delayed, 44-45; dissolved, 45-46
—Fifth: called, 45-46;

leadership in, 55-56; asks for separation, 56
—Sixth: organized, 62; time limit expired, 63; anger over delay, 63; provides for Seventh Convention, 64; thanks to John Brown, 65
—Seventh: election for, 67; organizes, 67; requests enabling act, 68; Wilkinson seeks separation, 68-69; addresses to Congress and General Assembly, 70-71
—Eighth: organizes, 77; rejects Third Enabling Act, 78-79; requests Indian protection, 79-80
—Ninth: organizes, 86-87; requests separation, 87; addresses to Congress and General Assembly, 88-89; provides for constitutional convention, 89-90
—Tenth: preliminary discussion, 97-103; delegates selected, 103-4; organized, 104; on form of government, 105-8; debate on slavery, 108-11; drafting committee, 112-13. *See also* Constitution, Kentucky, of 1792; Nicholas, George

Conway, Miles W., 133
Conway Cabal: and James Wilkinson, 35
coroners: election of, 123
Cotterill, R.S., 21
counties: on Virginia frontier, 9; Kentucky County created, 9; new counties in 1792, 146. *See also individual counties by name*
country faction: described, 22-23; favors U.S. constitution, 58

court faction: described, 22-24; economic aims, 24; and unilateral separation, 43; dominates Fifth Convention, 56; opposes U.S. constitution, 57-58; Muter deserts, 65-66; opposes separation, 74; missing in Ninth Convention, 86. *See also* Spanish Conspiracy; Wilkinson, James

Court of Appeals, 122, 123, 141, 144; and land jurisdiction, 144

Court of Oyer and Terminer, 141, 145

courts: created in District of Kentucky, 10; county, 10, 144-45; federal district, 10, 75; court of land commissioners, 11; appeal problems, 15; District's Supreme Court, 28; considered at Tenth Convention, 106-7; in 1792 constitution, 122-23, 141; established by General Assembly, 144-45. *See also* Court of Appeals

Coward, Joan, 92

Crab Orchard, 91

Craig, John, 133

Craig, Lewis: describes Kentucky, 5; and Travelling Church, 7

Cravens, Jeff, 132

Crawford, James, 111

Crockett, Joseph, 78-79, 132

Crow's Station. *See* Danville

Cumberland Gap, 8, 14, 91

Cumberland settlements, 56

Daniel, Walker, 24, 25

Danville, 14, 25, 137-38

Danville Political Club, 44-45; on constitutions, 95-96

Davis, James, 87, 132

debt: authorized in 1792, 144

Delany's Ferry, 147

Devine, Roger, 104, 139

"Disinterested Citizen" (George Nicholas?), 102

District of Kentucky, 9

Dorsey, Greenbury, 137

Dunn, Isaac, 53

Eastin, Richard, 133

education: missing in 1792 constitution, 128; early schools, 128; system advocated, 128-29

Edwards, John, 23, 67, 69, 132, 147; urges restraint, 63-64; elected U.S. senator, 146

elections: in 1792, 131-34; disputed, 143. *See also* conventions, in Kentucky; Marshall, Humphrey; Wilkinson, James

emancipation: in Tenth Convention, 108-11; in constitution, 125. *See also* Rice, Rev. David; slavery

enabling acts: first, 41-42; second, 45-46, 56, 62, 73; third, 73-74, 78-79; fourth, 80-81, 104. *See also* Virginia Compact

Executive Council of Virginia, 1-2; opposed in 1792, 106

factions: described, 21-24. *See also* country faction; court faction; partisan faction

Falls of the Ohio. *See* Louisville

Fayette County, 9, 126, 132, 147

Federalist Papers, 116

"Felte Firebrand," 100

First Memorial, 49-50. *See also* Wilkinson, James

Fleming, William, 6, 20, 25, 26

Floyd, John, 7
Fowler, John, 56, 71, 84
Fox, Arthur, 143
Frankfort, 147-48
Franklin, proposed state of, 46
French and Indian War, 3
Frowman, Jacob, 132
Frye, Benjamin, 143

Galloway, Joseph, 13-14
Gano, Rev. John, 138, 139, 146
Gardoqui, Don Diego de, 18, 62, 68-69, 72. *See also* Jay-Gardoqui Treaty
Garrard, James, 84, 87, 88, 89, 103, 105, 108, 110, 111, 112, 113
Gass, Thomas, 132
Gayoso, Manuel, 81
General Assembly, Kentucky, 1792: organizes, 138-39, 142; and Shelby, 139-42; evaluation of, 142; legislative routine, 142; changes in membership, 142-43; bills passed, 143-46; pay of, 145-46; counties created by, 146; and selection of capital, 146-48; adjourns, 148
governor: Nicholas's views on, 106; office of, 119-21. *See also* Shelby, Isaac
Grant, John, 133
Great Britain: and westward movement, 5
Green, Willis, 29
Green River military lands, 11
Greenup, Christopher, 16, 26, 44, 132, 137; on Court of Oyer and Terminer, 141
Gregg, John, 133
grievances. *See* conventions
Grubbs, Higgarson, 132

Hallock, Thomas, 133
Hardin, John, 141

Harris, Christopher, Jr., 132
Harris, Jordan: affair with Humphrey Marshall, 58-59
Harrison, Benjamin, 132, 141
Harrison, Governor Benjamin, 24
Harrison, Cuthbert, 112, 133
Harrod, James, 6
Harrodsburg, 1, 25, 128
Hawkins, John, 132
Henderson, Richard, 2-3. *See also* Transylvania Company
Henry, Patrick, 1, 44, 59, 94
Hobbs, Joseph, 133
Hobbs, Joshua, 133, 143
Holmes, Andrew: donations for state capital, 147, 148
Hood, Andrew, 133
houses: changes in, 92
"H.S.B.M.," 100, 101

immigration: national origins, 5-6, 7; change in, 7-9; routes into Kentucky, 8; into Spanish territory, 50
impeachment, 122
Indians, 20; treaties with, 2, 3; dangers from, 15, 24-25; campaign of 1786 against, 44-45; need for protection from, 75, 79-80, 82, 91. *See also* Cherokees; Chickamaugas
Innes, Harry, 10, 24, 31, 35, 44, 46, 47, 56, 63, 67-68, 72, 84, 132, 137; corresponds with Washington, 77; handles Wilkinson's affairs, 86; on human nature, 96; on constitution making, 99-100; in Tenth Convention, 103, 112; on Court of Appeals, 141
Ireland, Robert, 145
Irvin, William, 132
Irvine, Christopher, 26

Jachman, Richard, 132
Jay, John, 18, 46
Jay-Gardoqui Treaty, 18, 46
Jefferson, Thomas, 13, 56, 59, 94, 95
Jefferson County, 9, 30, 133, 138-39
Johnson, David, 138
Johnson, Robert, 84, 133, 134
Jones, John Gabriel, 1
Jones, Thomas, 133
Jouett, John, 132
justices of the peace, 144-45

Kavenaugh, Charles, 111
Kennedy, Thomas, 112, 134, 147
Kentucky County: created, 3, 9; described, 5; becomes District of Kentucky, 9
Kentucky Gazette, 56, 58, 65, 74, 90, 91, 92, 128, 129; founded, 54-55; and discussion of a constitution, 97-103. *See also* Bradford, John
Kentucky River, 147
Kentucky Society for Promoting Manufactures, 92
King, William, 133
King's Mountain, battle of, 134, 137
Knox, James, 143

land: desire for, 7; types of claims, 7, 10-11; Virginia laws, 11-12, 16; ownership of, 12; suits over, 16; after separation, 41-42; required for Virginia suffrage, 64-65; in Virginia compact, 80-81. *See also* country faction; partisan faction
land cases: jurisdiction of Court of Appeals, 107
laws: at Boonesborough, 2; enacted in 1792, 143-46

lawyers: effort to exclude from legislature, 100-101; in Tenth Convention, 103, 106
leadership: in separation movement, 8-9; change in, 19-20; of Benjamin Logan, 19-20; doubted in 1792, 93-95; in Tenth Convention, 96-97. *See also* Nicholas, George; Shelby, Isaac; Wilkinson, James
Ledgerwood's Bend, 147
Lee, Henry, 84, 147
Leestown, 147
legislature: Nicholas on form of, 105-6; in constitution, 118-20. *See also* General Assembly
Letcher, Benjamin, 132
Lewis, Nicholas, 139
Lewis, Thomas, 132, 138
Lexington, 9, 92, 147, 148
Lincoln County, 9, 132, 146
"Little Brutus," 101
Logan, Benjamin, 6, 26, 31, 46, 56, 84, 86-87, 88, 103, 132; opposes Henderson, 3; leadership of, 9; described, 19-20; and Indian campaign of 1786, 44-45; major-general of militia, 141
Logan, John, 132, 134, 143, 146
Logan County, 146
London Company: 1609 charter, 3
Lord Dunmore's War, 134
Louisville, 7, 147

McClung, John A., 8
McDowell, John, 132
McDowell, Samuel, 24, 26, 28, 31, 34, 41, 44, 46, 55, 56, 62-63, 67, 71, 77, 86, 103, 104, 112, 113-14; on Court of Oyer and Terminer, 141. *See also* conventions in Kentucky

200 *Index*

McDowell, William, 134, 141, 143
McIntosh, General Lachan, 7
McKay, James, 132
McKay, Kenneth, 138
McKenny, John, 133
Madison, Gabriel, 132
Madison, James, 26, 34, 38, 41, 42, 81, 94, 96, 97, 126, 130: opposes Jay-Gardoqui Treaty, 46; on ratification of U.S. constitution, 59-60; fears Spanish connection, 74; on best form of government, 95
Madison County, 9, 132
manufacturing, 79, 92
Marshall, Humphrey, 32, 36, 55, 71, 84; described, 23; first historian, 23; defeated for Fourth Convention, 43-44; and Virginia's ratifying convention, 58-59, 61; affair with Jordan Harris, 58-59; quoted, 63; on Tenth Convention, 103
Marshall, James, 88, 89
Marshall, John, 44, 59; on separation, 16-17
Marshall, Thomas, 71, 77, 96; leader of country faction, 23; and George Muter, 66
Martin, John, 132
Mason, George, 94; opposes U.S. constitution, 59
Mason County, 133
Maxwell, John, 132
May, John, 25
May, William, 133
Mercer County, 9, 75, 78, 107, 126, 132, 147
militia, 141
Miller, John, 132
ministers: at Tenth Convention, 103, 108, 110-11, 113. *See also* Craig, Lewis; Gano, Rev. John;

Garrard, James; Rice, Rev. David
Miro, Esteban Rodriguez: governor of Louisiana, 49; and Wilkinson's first trip, 49-50; doubts Wilkinson, 54; and colonization, 72; Wilkinson's second trip, 82-86. *See also* Spanish Conspiracy; Wilkinson, James
Mississippi River: use of, restricted, 17-18, 41, 48, 53, 68, 75; opened to Wilkinson, 50; opened to trade, 85. *See also* Jay-Gardoqui Treaty; Spanish Conspiracy; Wilkinson, James
Monroe, James, 38, 41
Montgomery, William, 87, 132, 141
Moore, William, 25
Mosby, Robert, 132, 143
Muter, George, 20, 23, 31, 34, 35, 41, 42, 44, 46, 47, 67, 71, 78, 84, 104, 133; issues handbill, 65-66; described, 66; president of Ninth Convention, 86; heads Court of Oyer and Terminer, 141, 145

Natchez, 49
Nelson County, 9, 30, 133
New Orleans, 49
Nicholas, George: favors ratification of U.S. constitution, 59, 60; described, 74-75; and conditions in Kentucky in 1789, 75-77, 81-82; father of 1792 constitution, 96, 111; forsakes politics, 96; elected to Tenth Convention, 97, 103-4; opening address, 105; on legislature, 105-6; on

executive, 106; on suffrage, 106, 121-22; on judiciary, 106-7; defends legal system, 107; resigns from convention, is reelected, 107-8; defends slavery, 109-10; drafts constitution, 112-13; on land cases, 123; on holding another convention, 126; on constitution, 130; appointed attorney general, 141
Northwest Ordinance of 1787, 91

oath of office, 124
O'Fallon, Dr. James, 85
Ohio River, 42, 91; route to Kentucky, 8
Orr, Alexander, 133, 134, 143

Paine, Thomas: author of *The Public Good*, 13
Paris, Kentucky, 146
partisan faction: described, 13-14, 21-22; in convention, 20, 55; opposes separation, 74, 80; dislike of lawyers, 100-101
Patterson, Robert, 132
Pawling, Henry, 132, 143
Payne, Edward, 132
Pendleton, Edmund, 95
Pennsylvania constitutions (1776, 1790), 104, 116
pensions: suggested by Wilkinson, 84; sought for Wilkinson, 84-86; received, 179 n 18
Petersburg, 147
petitions: for separation, 12, 13, 17; opposing separation, 43, 44, 45, 80; on use of the Mississippi River, 68; opposing violent separation, 70; to Tenth Convention, 105

"Philanthropus": advocates system of education, 128-29
"Philip Philips": antislavery views, 101
Point Pleasant, battle of, 134
political parties: missing in Kentucky, 21. *See also* factions
Pomeroy, George, 13-14
Pope, Benjamin, 133
population: in 1784, 24; in 1788, 8; in 1790, 8, 91
printer: called for at First Convention, 27. *See also* Bradford, John
Proclamation of 1763, 3
Public Good, The, 13

Quarter Session Courts, 145

Randolph, Beverly, 79
Randolph, Edmund, 56, 59
Rankin, Robert, 133
ratification of U.S. constitution, 59-61
representation: in Virginia legislature, 9-10; by estimated population, 29; in 1792 constitution, 105-6, 111, 118
representatives, U.S., 146
revenue. *See* taxes
Rice, Rev. David, 108-9, 110
Richmond, 14
Roberts, Benjamin, 133
Rogers, James, 25
Russell, William, 132

"Salamander," 100-101
Scotch-Irish, 5-6, 7
Scott, Charles, 141
Scott, Samuel, 26
Scott County, 146
Sebastian, Benjamin, 24, 34, 44, 47, 56, 63, 67-68, 69, 72, 84, 86, 103, 112; on Court of Appeals, 141

Second Continental Congress, 3, 12

secretary of state for Kentucky, 120-21, 141

sectionalism, 60, 90; and admission of Kentucky, 61-62. *See also* Jay-Gardoqui Treaty

senators: state, in 1792 constitution, 106, 118; elected in 1792, 134; U.S., elected in 1792, 146

separation from Virginia: early threat of, 1; provided for in constitution, 4; options for, 4-5; causes of, 12, 13, 14-16; Thomas Paine advocates, 13; John Marshall on, 16-17; James Speed fears, 17; grievances at First Convention, 27-29; considered at Second Convention, 32; Wilkinson suggests to Spain, 49-50; debated, 55, 80; at Seventh Convention, 67-71; issue in 1789, 81-82; danger of, fades, 86; U.S. approves, 90; agreed to, 93. *See also* conventions in Kentucky; Spanish Conspiracy; Wilkinson, James

separation of powers: necessary in government, 102, 105, 106; principle violated by county courts, 145

Sheaf of Wheat Inn, 138

Shelby, Gen. Evan, 134

Shelby, Isaac, 9, 20, 26, 27, 64, 78, 84, 86-87, 88, 132; in Tenth Convention, 103, 105, 111-12; elected governor, 133, 137; career to 1792, 134, 137; inaugurated, 137-38; described, 139-40; addresses General Assembly, 140; relations with General Assembly, 141; makes appointments, 141

Shelby, Letitia Cox, 134

Shelby, Susannah, 137

Shelby County, 146

Shepherd, Adam, 133

sheriffs, 123

Shipp, Mr., 87

Short, Peyton, 44, 132, 134

slavery: in 1792, 91; debated before Tenth Convention, 101; in Kentucky, 108-9; considered in Tenth Convention, 109-11, 113; in Article IX in constitution, 125. *See also* antislavery; Nicholas, George; Rice, Rev. David

Smith, Charles, 133

Smith, George, 110

Smith, James, 110, 116, 133

South Carolina–Yazoo Land Company, 85

Spain: controls Mississippi River, 17. *See also* Jay-Gardoqui Treaty; Miro, Esteban; Spanish Conspiracy; Wilkinson, James

Spanish Conspiracy, 36, 47, 49-54, 68-69, 71-72, 74, 82-86. *See also* Miro, Esteban; Wilkinson, James

stations: life in, 6

Steele, William, 133, 143

Stockton, George, 133

Strong, Walter E., 132

suffrage: liberal, for Seventh Convention, 64-65; in Tenth Convention, 106; in 1792 constitution, 121-22

Sullivan, William, 133

Swope, Benedict, 111

Sycamore Shoals, Treaty of, 2

Talbot, Haile, 143

taxes: land, of 1782, 16;

protested, 28, 35; in First
Enabling Act, 41-42; in 1792,
143-44
Taylor, Hubbard, 94, 111, 132
Taylor, James, 21
Taylor, Richard, 84, 133
Taylor, Samuel, 22, 55, 77, 84,
132; opposes separation, 43,
74, 80; in Tenth Convention,
103, 110
Thomas, Edmund, 133
Thompson, George: on Indian
problems, 79-80, 91
Thruston, Buckner, 138
tobacco, 53, 143-44
Todd, Levi, 25
Todd, Richard, 134
Todd, Robert, 132, 141, 147
Todd, Thomas, 44, 132, 139;
clerk of conventions, 31, 34,
55, 62, 67, 77, 86, 104, 105
Tories, 6
"To the Inhabitants of the
District of Kentucky," 36-38
towns, 9. *See* Danville;
Frankfort; Lexington;
Louisville
trade: with Spanish
possessions, 48-49; Wilkin-
son's concession, 50, 53-54; on
Mississippi River, 53
Transylvania Company, 2-3
Transylvania Seminary, 27, 108,
128
travel: dangers of, 14-15, 91;
defined for payments, 145.
See also Cumberland Gap;
Ohio River
Traveller's Rest, 137
Travelling Church, 7
treasurer, 120, 146
treaties: of Sycamore Shoals, 2;
of Fort Stanwick, 3; Jay-
Gardoqui, 46
Trotter, James, 132

Vermont, 90
Virginia Compact. *See* enabling
acts, fourth
Virginia constitution, 1776, 4
Virginia ratifying convention,
1788, 57-61
voting: for Fourth Convention,
43-44; Madison's advice on,
95; suggested by Danville
Political Club, 96; and
partisan faction, 98-99; in
Tenth Convention, 106; for
governor, 133. *See also*
suffrage

Wallace, Caleb, 7, 14, 20, 24, 26,
28, 31, 71; on Supreme Court
of District of Kentucky, 32, 34;
on work of Third Convention,
38; favors separation, 55, 67;
on Court of Appeals, 141
Waller, John, 132
Walsont, Matthew, 60
Walton, Matthew, 133
Waring, Thomas, 112
Washington, George, 35, 59-60;
concerned about Kentucky,
77; recommends admission, 90
Watkins, John, 133
Watlington, Patricia, 21, 172 n 7
Wilderness Trace, 2, 14, 91
Wilkinson, Ann Biddle, 9, 50
Wilkinson, James, 103, 147;
leader in court faction, 24;
previous career, 35; described,
36; opposes First Enabling
Act, 43; in Fourth Convention,
43-44; first New Orleans trip,
49-51; and start of Spanish
Conspiracy, 49-53; First
Memorial, 49-50; pushes
Spanish Conspiracy, 51, 53;
suspicions of, 54; describes
John Brown, 57; in Sixth
Convention, 63; plans for

Seventh Convention, 66-67; in
Seventh Convention, 67-72;
colonization scheme, 72;
second new Orleans trip,
82-85; Second Memorial,
82-84; seeks rewards, 83-84;
list of Kentuckians to be
bribed, 84; economic plight
of, 85-86; secures army
comission, leaves Kentucky,
86; receives Spanish pension,
179 n 18. *See also* Spanish
Conspiracy

William and Mary, College of,
27, 56, 74
"Will Wisp," 100
Wilson, John, 133
Wood, William, 84
Woodford County, 133
Woodford Courthouse, 146
Wythe, George, 56, 94

"X.Y.Z.," 102

Yazoo River, 72
Young, Richard, 133